MENTAL HEALTH MATTERS

UNDERSTANDING OCD

JENNIFER LOMBARDO

ROSEN PUBLISHING

Published in 2026 by The Rosen Publishing Group, Inc.
2544 Clinton Street, Buffalo, NY 14224

Portions of this work were originally authored by Jacqueline Adams and published as *Obsessive-Compulsive Disorder*. All new material this edition authored by Jennifer Lombardo.

Cataloging-in-Publication Data

Names: Lombardo, Jennifer.
Title: Understanding OCD / Jennifer Lombardo.
Description: First edition. | Buffalo, NY : Rosen Publishing, 2026. | Series: Mental health matters | Includes glossary and index.
Identifiers: ISBN 9781499479607 (pbk.) | ISBN 9781499479614 (library bound) | ISBN 9781499479621 (ebook)
Subjects: LCSH: Obsessive-compulsive disorder--Juvenile literature.
Classification: LCC RC533.L66 2026 | DDC 616.85'227--dc23

Manufactured in the United States of America

CPSIA Compliance Information: Batch #CSRYA26. For further information, contact Rosen Publishing at 1-800-237-9932.

CONTENTS

FOREWORD

There are many misconceptions about illness, especially mental illness. Advances in scientific knowledge have increased our understanding of many diseases and disorders, including the common cold, diabetes, and cancer. Many of these sicknesses and chronic conditions cause physical symptoms that people can see and understand, and their causes are often easy to explain.

The same cannot always be said for mental illnesses. Mental disorders are just as common as physical disorders, but without physical symptoms, they are often dismissed. People tend to believe that a mental illness is easy to get over with enough willpower. They may call people with mental illnesses names such as "lazy" and "attention-seeking." Some people even deny that mental illnesses exist at all.

People who have been convinced by those around them that they have a problem of willpower rather than a treatable illness often go undiagnosed for years. This can cause a lot of suffering; people with an undiagnosed mental disorder often understand that they are experiencing the world in a different way than their peers, but they have no one to turn to for answers. Many feel guilty about not being able to control their symptoms, not realizing that this is as impractical as telling someone with a broken leg that they should be able to walk without pain if they simply try hard enough.

In recent years, the stigma, or perceived shame, of mental illness has decreased. More people, especially young people, are willing to seek therapy and talk openly about their diagnosed mental illnesses. However, this has also led to a rise in misinformation, which can be spread through personal anecdotes, social media, and even news sources. The misuse of "therapy speak" and armchair diagnoses by internet commenters are two growing problems. Furthermore, although the stigma has lessened, it has not disappeared completely. People sometimes use mental illnesses as insults. Someone who displays normal ranges of emotion, for example, may be called "bipolar" as an insult. This shows a lack of understanding about bipolar disorder and furthers the stigma around this disorder by making it sound like a negative aspect of who a person is.

This series aims to offer accurate information about mental illnesses so young adults will have a better understanding of them. Each volume discusses the symptoms of a particular illness, ways it is currently being treated, and the research that is being done to understand it further. Advice for people who may be suffering from a disorder is included, as well as information for their loved ones about how best to support them.

With fully cited quotes, a list of recommended books and websites for further research, and informational charts, this series provides young adults with a factual introduction to common mental illnesses. By learning more about these disorders, they will be better able to show compassion to people who are dealing with mental illnesses and take charge of their own mental health.

INTRUSIVE THOUGHTS

Obsessive-compulsive disorder (OCD) is a common but frequently misunderstood mental illness. It affects everyone who has it slightly differently, and its severity can change without warning. For example, spoken word artist Tiffany Dawn Hasse grew up with mild OCD that was nearly dormant for many years. However, seemingly overnight, Hasse had a severe onset of the disorder that nearly paralyzed her. "I'd just had my wisdom teeth removed and was immediately bombarded with incessant and intrusive unwanted thoughts,"[1] Hasse wrote. She added that these thoughts even included if she was actually seeing the sky as a blue color.

These thoughts prevented her from functioning as she had before, and she wrote, "Thoughts that didn't even matter and held no significance were debilitating; they prevented me from accomplishing the most mundane tasks. Tying my shoe only to untie it repetitively … spending long hours in a bathroom engaging in compulsive rituals such as tapping inanimate objects endlessly with no resolution … were just a few of the consequences I endured."[2] Her story is one that millions of people can relate to.

STAYING QUIET

One big misunderstanding about OCD involves how common it is. Until recently, experts believed OCD was a rare disorder. However, recent studies have shown that between 1 and 3 percent of Americans will develop OCD at some point in their life. One possible reason for this misunderstanding is that many people with OCD suffer in silence, believing that no one else will understand them and that no help is available.

Even if people with OCD decide to seek help, further misunderstandings can complicate the process. Because OCD is easily confused with disorders that have similar symptoms, such as depression, schizophrenia, and anxiety disorders, the process of getting an accurate diagnosis often takes years. Even after diagnosis, finding appropriate treatment is a challenge because providers may try techniques that are helpful for other mental disorders but are ineffective—or even damaging—for someone with OCD.

OCD is much more complex and complicated than how it is often portrayed in the media. For example, most fictional depictions of someone with OCD focus on compulsive cleaning. While this is often a symptom of a kind of OCD called contamination OCD, it is not the only way this disorder presents itself.

MAKING IT WORSE

Mistaken ideas among loved ones of people with OCD can contribute to the problem. Family members and friends who believe that people with OCD could simply stop their behavior if they really wanted to do so may react with criticism and frustration. This only raises the person's anxiety, which in turn increases their symptoms. On the opposite end of the spectrum, some loved ones imagine that they are helping those with OCD by taking part in compulsive rituals that temporarily relieve anxiety. For example, some family members accommodate demands that they hose off in the garage before entering the house or that they participate in reassurance rituals by answering the same question over and over because they believe they are helping their loved one with OCD. However, rather than helping those with OCD, accommodating OCD compulsions ultimately makes the anxiety worse and allows the sufferer to continue their unhealthy behavior patterns. It may even prevent them from seeking help.

People with OCD and their loved ones also experience frustration when people misunderstand the disorder. With increased media coverage, many people today have heard of OCD, but they often misunderstand its nature. They fail to comprehend the time-consuming mental rituals and underlying anxiety that consume the lives of people with OCD. As Hasse wrote, "My obsessive thoughts were gripping, incessant, and utterly bizarre … I was worried about things that made no intellectual sense such as whether or not my zipper, if zipped improperly, could correlate to something bad happening to my family."[3]

In addition, people may assume certain things about the disorder—they may think that all highly organized people have OCD or that all people with OCD wash their hands a lot. However, each person's symptoms are unique, and the disorder is much more serious than just a desire for things to be organized. In fact, OCD can be debilitating.

Most people enjoy having a tidy workspace. This alone is not a sign of OCD.

GETTING THROUGH IT

While OCD can be debilitating, those with the disorder find ways to get through each moment. For example, Hasse and others use creative outlets along with therapies to help them. There is no single correct approach to treat the disorder. Just as each person's symptoms are unique to them, the treatment that works best for them is also unique. As medical technologies advance, doctors are continuing to find ways to potentially treat the disorder, while celebrities such as Maria Bamford, John Green, Ariana Grande, and others are increasing awareness of the disorder.

CHAPTER ONE

OBSESSIONS AND COMPULSIONS

Obsessive-compulsive disorder is accurately named: It is a mental health disorder that involves obsessive thoughts and compulsions that are used to try to dispel those distressing thoughts. Obsessive thoughts are irrational, unwanted thoughts that repeatedly play over and over in a person's head. Even if the person knows the thoughts do not make sense, they have trouble believing the thoughts are not true.

Compulsions are the person's attempt to keep the thoughts from coming true or to convince themselves that the thoughts are indeed irrational. Repetitive rituals, such as washing, counting, and ruminating, give the person relief for a brief time but never a sense of long-term satisfaction, which is why the behaviors continue. While most people have experienced obsessive thoughts or compulsive behaviors at one time or another, if a person experiences them for more than an hour a day and they get in the way of the person's ability to live their life, they probably have OCD.

In simple terms, a person with OCD becomes caught in a cycle of obsessions and compulsions that they are unable to stop and do not enjoy. These compulsions and obsessions are time-consuming and get in the way of activities the person enjoys.

According to the International OCD Foundation (IOCDF), obsessions and compulsions getting in the way of daily activities is one of the most important factors in determining whether someone has a psychological disorder.

CLINICAL OBSESSION

"Obsessed" is a word that is commonly used in everyday language. It is casually used for a variety of things, such as being "obsessed" with fashion or *Star Wars*. It is important to emphasize the difference between obsession that is clinical, or indicative of a mental illness, and the casual term that is used in everyday language. The casual use of the term means someone is preoccupied with a piece of media, a topic or interest, or even a person. However, these people are still able to go about their daily activities—they can make it to work or school on time, meet up with friends, and talk about a variety of topics despite having this "obsession."

Someone who is clinically diagnosed with OCD, however, finds these normal daily activities interrupted. They have obsessive thoughts combined with compulsions to attempt to make their obsessions go away. Unlike someone who is "obsessed" with a television show or song, they do not have a choice in their obsessions, and the themes of the obsessions tend to be incredibly unpleasant. For example, someone may obsess that they will lose their job or somehow commit a crime by accident.

The usage of the word "obsession" in an everyday sense to describe how much one likes something can be harmful to those with OCD. According to the IOCDF, "Individuals with OCD have a hard time hearing this usage of 'obsession' as it feels as though it diminishes their struggle with OCD symptoms."[4]

EXAMPLES OF OCD

While each person with OCD has a unique experience with the disorder, there are some typical obsessions and compulsions that occur. These may include:

Typical Obsessions in OCD

- fear of causing physical harm to self or others
- fear of contamination
- doubt that an action has been performed
- disturbing mental images
- belief that bad thoughts can cause harm to others
- doubt about one's beliefs

Typical Compulsions in OCD

- cleaning
- checking
- putting objects or possessions in a strict order
- searching the internet for answers
- repeating a mental or physical ritual to counteract a bad thought
- asking for repeated assurances

GRAPPLING WITH DOUBT

Obsessions can take many forms and generally involve intrusive, or sudden and unwanted, fears that something harmful will happen or doubts over whether something harmful has already happened. Fear of contamination is one of the most common. People with this fear believe they will be harmed by contact with dirt and germs, or they worry that they are somehow contaminated and may pass this along to others, directly or indirectly. Another common obsession is doubt that they have performed some necessary action, such as locking the doors or checking the knobs on the stove. They worry that they or others will be harmed as a result of their carelessness.

Intrusive thoughts can take the form of repeated disturbing images. They can also arise as urges to do something aggressive, such as harming someone, or humiliating, such as shouting obscenities in public.

People with OCD do not act on these unwanted urges, but they worry excessively that they might. They also worry that these urges might reflect unconscious desires, when the opposite is the case. Psychologist Fred Penzel wrote, "For reasons we don't yet understand, some people's obsessive thoughts seem to latch onto whatever they may find most repulsive or disgusting."[5]

Most people realize that their intrusive, obsessive thoughts are irrational, but they cannot stop them or ignore them. OCD has been called "the doubting sickness" because people with OCD seem unable to believe what their senses tell them. They may see that the door is locked, but they still doubt that they have locked it once it is out of their sight, so they may check it repeatedly to make sure their memory is not faulty. They may see no dirt on their hands after washing, but they still do not believe that they are clean. Former professional hockey player Clint Malarchuk, whose struggle with OCD began when he was a child, explained these doubts:

> *I could say this table is brown. I know it's brown and you know it's brown. But when you're obsessing, you get stuck. You don't believe it. You can actually say, "Yeah, I know it's brown." But up here, in your head, it just doesn't finish. You can't finish your thought. It's like stuttering. It's the same sort of thing. When somebody is stuttering and he's stuck, it's not so much the physical part of the mouth not being able to finish the word. It's a mental thing.*[6]

COMMON COMPULSIONS

This overwhelming doubt leads to great anxiety. People may respond to this anxiety by avoiding the objects or situations they fear. A person obsessed with fear of contamination may avoid public restrooms, or a person troubled by an unwanted urge to shout obscenities in inappropriate places may avoid going to church. People with OCD also cope by performing compulsions—physical or mental rituals they believe will prevent the feared event from happening. Most realize the rituals are excessive or irrational, but they feel compelled to perform them to relieve their anxiety.

Obsessions and compulsions are not always logically related. For example, someone may flip a light switch on and off a specific number of times to get rid of an unwanted thought in their head about harming someone in their family.

Cleaning and checking are among the most common compulsions. People obsessed with fear of contamination may spend hours a day cleaning their homes or washing themselves. In extreme cases, a person may not let visitors into their homes or may insist that family members change their clothes before coming inside. Sometimes a compulsion is more symbolically related to an obsession. For example, people with OCD may perform cleaning compulsions to wash away guilt rather than physical dirt or germs.

Those with checking compulsions may spend time locking and relocking doors or checking and rechecking appliances out of fear that a burglar will get in or a fire will start. Once leaving the house, they may have to go back many times to check again. When driving, some feel compelled to retrace their route over and over to check that they did not hit a pedestrian along the way.

Another form of checking is for the person with OCD to repeatedly ask for assurances that they have not caused some type of harm, with the result that friends and family may become frustrated at answering the same question dozens of times, only to have the question asked again. Often, doctors unknowingly become involved in this type of ritual as patients repeatedly ask them for reassurances about their health.

Reassurance-seeking can sometimes be subtle. For instance, someone with OCD who worries that they may have somehow harmed a visitor to their home may find repeated excuses to call the person in the days following the visit. They may not ask about their fears directly, but if the visitor sounds fine on the phone, this provides assurance that they caused them no harm. A driver who is plagued by doubts over hitting pedestrians may ask another person to ride along so that the passenger's reactions can be observed without their knowledge. If the driver hits a bump and the passenger acts as if everything is normal, this provides assurance that nothing bad has happened.

OTHER TYPES OF COMPULSIONS

Besides cleaning and checking, many other types of compulsions exist. Some people spend time arranging possessions or furniture in a certain order and become very upset when an item is moved. According to Penzel, "Sloppiness and asymmetry seem to bother and offend them. If they see things that do not look properly ordered or arranged, they will find themselves thinking about them continuously and often cannot get on with other business until something has been done about it."[7] A variation of this need for order compels some to start their work over and over again in an effort to make it perfect. As a result, some students find themselves unable to complete homework assignments and their grades fall.

Some compulsions arise from an obsessive belief that thinking about something can cause it to happen; for example, a bad thought about a family member can bring harm to that person. Those with OCD often repeat a ritual over and over in an effort to undo or counteract the unwanted thought. The repeated action can be mental, such as a prayer, or physical, such as entering and reentering a room until it feels "right." Some people with OCD feel the need to perform actions a certain number of times or to count up to a "good" number to cancel out a "bad" number.

Some compulsions do not connect logically to the event they are designed to prevent. For example, someone may touch a doorway in a certain manner when passing through to prevent harm from coming to a family member. Compulsions that are connected to the obsessions are performed to an excessive degree; for example, people obsessed with fears of contamination may scrub their hands hundreds of times a day, to the point that their skin bleeds. Although people with OCD perform compulsions to gain relief from anxiety, these rituals bring no lasting peace. Instead, they cause added stress. These rituals may consume so much time that people find it difficult to get to work or bed on time or even to leave the house.

Some people struggle with one type of OCD, while others experience a variety of symptoms. A woman

ON THE OCD SPECTRUM

After much debate among researchers, in 2013, the *Diagnostic and Statistical Manual of Mental Disorders, Fifth Edition* (*DSM-5*) included hoarding disorder under the category of Obsessive-Compulsive and Related Disorders (OCRDs). Compulsive hoarders often fear that if they get rid of an object, they or someone else will later need it. Some hoarders feel an emotional attachment to the items they collect. These may fill a room until it has to be closed off, after which the clutter begins to fill the next room. To others, these items may seem to have little or no value. They commonly include papers—not only important documents but also junk mail and newspapers—broken items, and clothing. The health department or the code enforcement division of the police department must sometimes step in to assess health or fire hazards.

The symptoms that make hoarding similar to OCD are repetitive thoughts, negative emotions, and compulsive behaviors, but each has its unique features. People with OCD have irrational beliefs, while people with hoarding disorder have distorted beliefs, which do often have a basis for rationale. For instance, while being resourceful is a good thing, believing that nothing should ever be thrown away is a distortion of that belief.

Another difference in someone with hoarding disorder versus someone with OCD is their lack of insight, or awareness that they have a mental illness. This, along with the distorted beliefs, makes treatment more difficult than in someone with OCD. The person with hoarding disorder cannot be convinced that being thrifty is wrong because being thrifty is a normal, acceptable behavior. They are unable to to see the extremeness of their behavior and recognize it as harmful, so there is no motivation to get help.

named Liz's battle with OCD began at age 12 with a compulsive need to wash her hair over and over. This escalated into a four-hour ritual that included the need to think "good thoughts." She remembered, "I would wash a section of my hair and if I thought of something bad then I would have to re-wash the area and think something good. This is the primary reason the showers took so long! I felt highly anxious at the time—it was a miserable experience."[8]

HISTORICAL CASES

Cases of suffering with these symptoms were documented long before doctors recognized the disorder now known as OCD. In the 17th century, priests described people who struggled with obsessive thoughts. Referring to one such case, scholar Robert Burton wrote in 1621, "If he be in a silent auditory, as at a sermon, he is afraid he shall speak aloud and unaware, something indecent, unfit to be said."[9]

At that time, obsessions and compulsions were described as symptoms of religious melancholy. John Moore, the bishop of Norwich, England, spoke of the problem when he described people who were obsessed by blasphemous thoughts, and "the more they struggle with them, the more they [increase]."[10]

Several famous historical figures suffered from symptoms that today's psychologists recognize as OCD. Fears of urges to speak blasphemies tormented John Bunyan, author of *Pilgrim's Progress*. He wrote that these urges were so strong "that often I have been ready to clap my hand under my chin, to hold my mouth from opening."[11]

Friends of 18th-century poet and writer Samuel Johnson observed that when he walked along a street, he never stepped on cracks. He touched every post as he passed it, and if he missed one, he felt compelled to go back and touch it while his friends waited. James Boswell, Johnson's biographer, wrote:

> *He had another peculiarity, of which none of his friends even ventured to ask an explanation. It appeared to me some superstitious habit, which he had contracted early, and from which he had never called upon his reason to disentangle himself. This was his anxious care to go out or in at a door or passage, by a certain number of steps from a certain point, or at least so as that either his right or his left foot (I am not certain which), should constantly*

> *make the first actual movement when he came close to the door or passage.*[12]

When billionaire Howard Hughes died in 1976, psychologist Raymond D. Fowler conducted a psychological autopsy, which included an examination of Hughes's communications and other documents and interviews with people who had known him. Fowler concluded that, among other problems, Hughes had suffered from OCD that progressively worsened throughout his life. Besides performing his own compulsive rituals, such as numerous touch-and-go landings in his airplane, Hughes required his employees to perform rituals for him. Fowler reported:

> *He made people who worked with him carry out elaborate hand-washing rituals and wear white cotton gloves, sometimes several pairs, when handling documents he would later touch. Newspapers had to be brought to him in stacks of three so he could slide the middle, and presumably least contaminated, copy out by grasping it with Kleenex. To escape contamination by dust, he ordered that masking tape be put around the doors and windows of his cars and houses.*[13]

Actor Leonardo DiCaprio played Howard Hughes in the 2004 movie *The Aviator*. DiCaprio also has OCD, and while it is normally controlled, he let that go in order to get into Hughes's character. DiCaprio's own symptoms of OCD involve stepping on cracks in the pavement and stepping on each gum stain he sees, sometimes walking backward to step on it to prevent something bad from happening. During filming, it would take him and his assistants several minutes to get to the set because of rituals he would have to perform to get there, such as touching doors a certain way, walking in and out of doors a certain way, and stepping on certain areas of the pavement.

Cleaning is an important chore. It only becomes a problem when it takes over a person's life.

NAMING THE DISORDER

Although symptoms had been reported for centuries, the disorder now known as OCD was not described in medical literature until 1838. Nineteenth-century psychiatrists debated whether it was a mental or an emotional disorder.

In the early 20th century, French psychologist and neurologist Pierre Janet and Austrian neurologist Sigmund Freud studied and wrote about the disorder. Over the following decades, treatment providers reported only a few cases of OCD. Freud's 1907 observation sheds light on a possible reason for this: "Sufferers from this illness are able to keep their affliction a private matter. Concealment is made easier from the fact that they are quite well able to fulfill their social duties during a part of the day, once they have devoted a number of hours to their secret doings, hidden from view."[14] Many suffered in secret out of embarrassment or fear that others would think they were crazy. Most of the public had never heard of the disorder. Until the 1980s, doctors believed OCD was very rare.

LEARNING MORE

Because of OCD's supposed rarity, psychiatrist Judith Rapoport anticipated that she would have a hard time finding enough people to participate in an OCD study she undertook in the 1970s. She wrote: "At the National Institute of Mental Health, I began the study thinking that it would take 10 years to see enough patients to get even an idea of the typical symptom patterns, the age at which they began, and what treatments worked."[15]

To her surprise, she received many calls from people with OCD and their parents. When she surveyed high school students, she learned that the disorder was much more common than previously thought.

In 1986, a group of people with OCD formed the Obsessive-Compulsive Foundation (OCF), an international organization that educates the public about OCD, helps those with OCD and their families, and supports research into causes and treatments of the disorder. As a result of their efforts to increase public awareness about OCD, the ABC news program *20/20* ran a report on it in 1987. For months, the study centers mentioned in the program received floods of calls and letters from people who had never known that their disorder had a name or that treatment was available. One caller said, "I was about to leave my wife. I thought she didn't care for us anymore. Now I know she is sick and just want her to get help."[16]

So many cases came to light that in 1989, psychologist Michael A. Jenike called OCD a "hidden epidemic."[17] Today, according to the IOCDF, 1 in 40 people have OCD or will develop it at some point in their life. The World Health Organization (WHO) ranked OCD as one of the top 20 causes of illness-related disability worldwide in people 15 to 44 years of age.

In the years since the *20/20* report, the OCF, which became the IOCDF, and other organizations have worked to increase awareness about OCD and its symptoms. However, there is still a wide divide between diagnosis and treatment of this disorder. Moderate cases of OCD are much less likely to be recognized by mental health professionals than severe cases, and then still, only a few of those who suffer from the severe cases receive treatment specifically for OCD.

Increased awareness of OCD also means celebrities have come out and acknowledged they have the disorder to further reduce the stigma, or negative view, that surrounds the disease. Even three decades ago, mental health was not something that was talked about. Former National Hockey League (NHL) player Corey Hirsch struggled for years with OCD before being diagnosed. In 2017, he wrote an article for *The Player's Tribune* about his experiences with the

People with OCD often feel embarrassed or scared to admit their intrusive thoughts, so they avoid seeking support.

disorder and stated that in his household in the 1990s, words such as "mental health" and "therapy" were not mentioned. According to Hirsch:

> *In our society, OCD has become shorthand for anybody who carries around a little bottle of hand sanitizer. Yes, compulsive hand-washing can be one of the signs of OCD. However, there are many different variations of OCD, and many of the compulsions are purely mental—you can't see the disease just by looking at a person …*

> *When you have OCD, your brain is not saying, "I want to do this horrible thing." Your brain is saying, "Oh my God,* what if *I did this horrible thing? How horrible would that be? … I hope I never do this." …*
>
> *People with OCD want 100% certainty. They want 100% certainty that they're not going to harm anyone. They want 100% certainty that they're not going to get some deadly disease. But their brain is lying to them—screaming at them, actually—that they're going to contract a deadly disease, and then they're going to [unintentionally] pass it on to their loved ones, and then it will be all their fault.*[18]

Hirsch struggled with OCD for years before being diagnosed. He added, "I am not insane. I am not a bad person. I am not weak. I have an illness, and there is a treatment."[19] It can take months or years for someone to receive an accurate diagnosis and figure out the treatment plan that is right for them.

DIAGNOSING OCD

Nearly all cases of OCD appear before someone turns 35. However, if someone is unaware of what their symptoms mean, it can be years before they are accurately diagnosed.

People who suffer from OCD often try to conceal their problem rather than ask for help. Many are so good at keeping their disorder a secret that they do not seek treatment for years, and by that time, the behaviors are so prevalent that they are much more difficult to change.

When they finally see a professional, they may be misdiagnosed at first. Many OCD symptoms are similar to other disorders, including anxiety disorder, depression, or schizophrenia. Also, many people have a dual diagnosis of OCD and another mental disorder, and it may take awhile for a mental health professional to realize that the person has more than one disorder.

Diagnosing and treating children with OCD is particularly difficult because sometimes the symptoms are treated but not the underlying cause. Children with OCD often have trouble with schoolwork, difficulty making decisions and concentrating, trouble with peers, and behavioral outbursts. Because of this, children with OCD are often misdiagnosed with depression, attention-deficit/hyperactivity disorder (ADHD), or behavioral problems.

WATERING DOWN OCD

A recent trend on social media involves people captioning a photo or video with the phrase "Letting my intrusive thoughts win." The photo or video typically shows the person doing something out of the ordinary, such as eating frosting straight from a piping bag, cutting their own hair, or doing a silly dance move in public.

People who suffer from OCD have pointed out that these are impulsive thoughts, not intrusive ones. Like intrusive thoughts, impulsive thoughts pop into a person's head seemingly out of nowhere. However, impulsive thoughts are silly, funny, or weird, while intrusive thoughts are disturbing, unwanted, and difficult to get rid of. In response to the trend, a new trend started in which people with OCD would compare others' so-called "intrusive" thoughts with their own, which were much darker and more dangerous—for example, thinking that they should jump off a high point, stalk someone they have a crush on, or run someone over with their car on purpose. Intrusive thoughts are typically thoughts a person has no desire to act on, while impulsive thoughts are ones they enjoy acting on. Confusing the two often makes people believe that someone with upsetting intrusive thoughts wishes to or is likely to act them out—the very thing OCD sufferers use compulsions to guard against.

People with OCD as well as mental health experts have pointed out that mental illnesses are not the same as personality traits or normal experiences that are common to all people. Most people have impulsive thoughts, like their home to be clean and organized, and have doubts that they have locked the door or turned off the stove. However, these become signs of a mental illness when they begin to seriously affect a person's life in a negative way.

Some people joke about having OCD in ways that water it down, or make it seem much less serious than it actually is. A person who spends an hour cleaning their home may say they are "a little bit OCD." This makes it seem as though OCD is a quirky personality trait, which makes it harder for people to understand why real OCD is so debilitating and upsetting to people who have it. When a person believes that OCD is simply the desire to have things around them clean and organized, they fail to understand the full impact of OCD on a person's life.

A DISTINCT DISORDER

The American Psychiatric Association's *Diagnostic and Statistical Manual of Mental Disorders* defines all known mental disorders and provides criteria for identifying them. The fifth edition, *DSM-5*, lists OCD in its own category, Obsessive-Compulsive and Related Disorders (OCRDs) for the first time, rather than defining it as an anxiety disorder as was done in previous publications.

First on the list of criteria for OCD is the existence of obsessions or compulsions that the person tries to ignore or suppress by using another thought or action to neutralize them. The *DSM-5* specifies that the person performs compulsions to reduce or prevent distress or to prevent a dreaded event or situation.

Although the criteria allow for either compulsions or obsessions, most people experience both. However, there are some people with OCD who experience what is known as primarily obsessional (sometimes also called primarily cognitive) OCD, nicknamed "pure-O." This form of the disorder is harder to diagnose and involves no outwardly visible rituals. Instead, people with pure-O OCD create rituals inside their heads, which may involve repeating a certain phrase over and over or counting to a certain number. They may ask themselves, 'What is the proof that I would not do this?' or 'How can I tell if I'm a psychopath?' They then ruminate, or think about those questions over and over, trying to find an answer that can give them 100 percent certainty.

OCD obsessions generally fall into four categories: violent thoughts, shameful sexual thoughts, disgusting thoughts, or blasphemous thoughts. Maria Bamford, stand-up comedian and voice actor for the cartoon *Adventure Time*, has OCD and has been outspoken about her experiences with it. In an interview with National Public Radio (NPR), she explained something commonly seen in people who have pure-O OCD:

> *When I was about 9 years old, I stopped being able to sleep at night 'cause I had a fear that I was going to ... act out violently in some sort of taboo way ... and so wanted to isolate so that I would not be around people at all and would stay up all night making sure that I just wouldn't fall asleep and somehow lose control ... It's the equivalent of ... washing your hands, thinking that you're going to be dirty or that you're somehow dirty, but it's with thoughts. So as soon as you try to not think of the thought, the thought pops up again.*[20]

Some people, such as Penzel, believe that pure-O OCD does not exist, and therefore there is a controversy over this form of the disorder. Penzel wrote, "Whenever a sufferer tells me that they are a 'Pure O,' I like to question them carefully about this. I have yet to run across anyone who actually belongs in this so-called category."[21] However, as a person with this type of OCD wrote on the website The Mighty, when people with pure-O OCD hear clinicians say pure-O does not exist, the "statement can be devastatingly triggering. When people hear 'Pure O' they sometimes think it means obsessions but no compulsions. But we actually have non-detectable mental compulsions."[22]

INTERFERING WITH LIFE

The *DSM-5* also lists other criteria for diagnosing OCD. The obsessions or compulsions must cause significant distress, consume more than one hour per day, and interfere with the person's life in a significant way.

The *DSM-5* also includes three insight levels. Someone with "good to fair insight" knows something

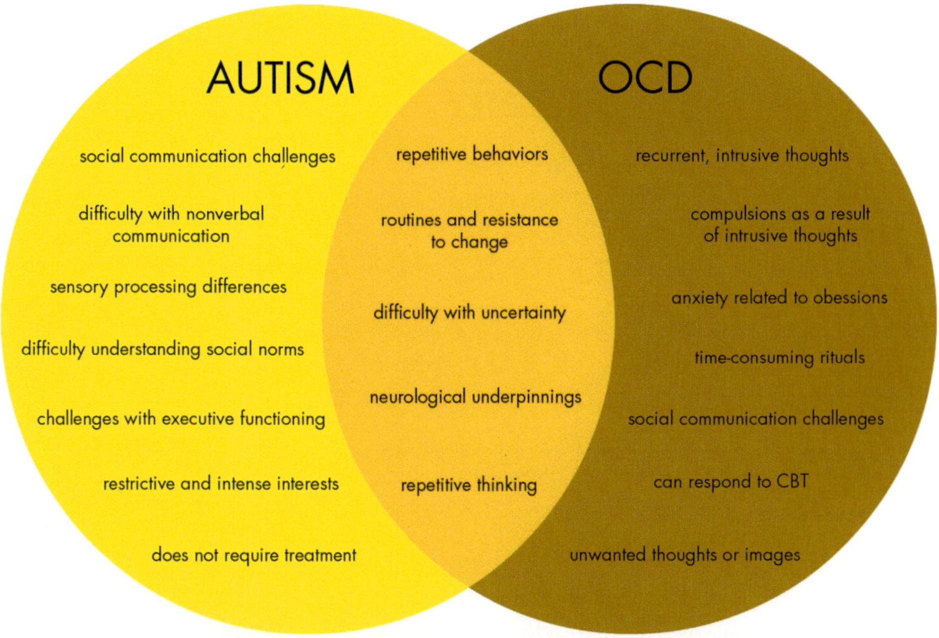

OCD can look similar to other disorders, such as autism spectrum disorder. Autism spectrum disorder does not require specific treatment, although therapies to manage the disorder may be helpful.

really is not going to happen even though they are compelled to perform a ritualistic behavior to prevent it. Someone with "poor insight" believes something bad might happen, and someone with "absent or delusional insight" is convinced that something bad is going to happen no matter how much evidence there is against it. In the past, people with absent or delusional insight were often misdiagnosed with a psychotic disorder. Psychiatric professionals hope that the clarification into insight might provide them with more accurate diagnoses.

Diagnosis of OCD may include a physical exam and lab testing to rule out any other medical conditions or substance abuse problems. A psychological evaluation is then done, generally in the form of an interview. The doctor will use the criteria in the *DSM-5* to determine whether or not the person has OCD.

DETERMINING SEVERITY

Other tools rate the range and severity of OCD symptoms. One of the most widely used is the Yale-Brown Obsessive Compulsive Scale (Y-BOCS) and Symptom Checklist. The checklist includes more than 60 different obsessions and compulsions. After reading definitions and examples of obsessions and compulsions to patients, the treatment provider then reads each item on the checklist. Patients say which ones they experience, whether those symptoms are current or in the past, and which ones are the strongest. The Y-BOCS is then used to rate time spent on, interference from, distress of, resistance, and control over both the obsessions and the compulsions. Besides initially rating the symptoms, the Y-BOCS also measures how the patients later respond to treatment. A children's version of the Y-BOCS, called the CY-BOCS, is also available.

Self-report forms, in which patients fill out a questionnaire, also help assess symptoms. Other commonly used self-report tools are the Obsessive Compulsive Inventory–Short Version and the Padua Inventory.

OCD symptoms can complicate the use of interviews and questionnaires. For instance, patients who believe that thinking or talking about a feared event makes it more likely to occur may have trouble discussing their obsessive fears. Patients with contamination obsessions may be distracted by a fear of handling the questionnaire. Patients with checking compulsions may have a hard time completing the questionnaire because they spend a lot of time asking about the meaning of the questions and checking and rechecking their answers. Psychologist Steven Taylor wrote, "For self-report measures, we encourage the patient to write down the first response that comes to mind, and discourage repeated checking of answers."[23] He reported that patience and persistent encouragement on the part of the doctor can help the patient overcome these challenges.

GAUGING AVOIDANCE

Treatment providers can also measure the severity of symptoms with behavioral avoidance tests (BATs). Patients are asked to move as close as possible to something that triggers anxiety, such as a garbage can in the case of people with contamination fears. Patients then rate their level of fear on a scale. The test may be repeated with other objects that cause anxiety, or it may be broken down into steps, with each step becoming more difficult.

An advantage of BATs is that they measure symptoms as they occur. BATs can be performed in

Questionnaires can help a mental health professional figure out how to approach treatment for someone with OCD. However, not all OCD patients need to complete this step to get effective care.

the treatment provider's office, or the provider can assign them as homework: The patient records levels of avoidance (based on how closely they can approach the object) and fear. BATs work well for contamination obsessions, but they are more difficult to use for symptoms such as checking and ordering.

RELATED DISORDERS

In the *DSM-5*, along with the familiar OCD diagnosis are two recently recognized disorders that have similar features to OCD: hoarding disorder and excoriation disorder (ED), also called skin picking. Other disorders related to OCD that are also included in this category are body dysmorphic disorder (BDD) and trichotillomania, or hair-pulling.

People with BDD become preoccupied with what they see as a physical defect in themselves, such as a crooked nose or a body part they believe is too big, too small, or misshapen. It may be an imagined or slight defect barely noticeable to others, but to the person with BDD, it is a source of extreme distress. Some avoid leaving their homes so no one else will see the perceived defect. They constantly check their appearance, asking others for reassurances, fixated on trying to hide the supposed defect. The main difference between BDD and OCD is that people generally have less insight about their condition.

Trichotillomania occurs when a person has a repeated urge to pull their own hair out. These people describe feelings of anxiety or tension that can only be relieved by pulling out hair from the scalp and eyebrows down to the legs. The feeling of relief is so great that it becomes a habit. The physical problems with pulling out one's hair—including baldness, infection, and skin damage—generally lead to emotional problems such as low self-esteem, embarrassment, and isolation.

People with trichotillomania, sometimes shortened to "trich," have a compulsion to pull their hair out. Left untreated, this can lead to things such as bald patches, sores, and infection.

Another change in the *DSM-5* is that when diagnosing someone with OCD, it should be noted whether the person has ever had a tic disorder. Tics are sudden, repeated motor movements or vocalizations, such as eye blinking, grunting, or shouting obscenities or insults. The person feels an irresistible urge to perform the action, and though they may try to suppress it, they eventually must perform the action to obtain relief. According to the Centers for Disease Control and Prevention (CDC), up to 30 percent of people diagnosed with OCD have had a tic disorder.

SKIN PICKING

The new diagnosis of ED in the *DSM-5* is characterized by repeatedly scratching, rubbing, or picking skin to the point of causing damage. The urge to pick is similar to OCD in that people with ED are trying to get rid of some sort of imperfection, such as a scab or acne, or sometimes a perceived imperfection below the skin. Many people with ED pick themselves with more intensity during stressful situations, and they

Many people feel the urge to pop their pimples. However, a person with ED cannot stop picking at their acne and other skin anomalies even if they are doing damage to their skin.

feel they cannot stop no matter how much damage has been done to their body. Eventually, many need medical treatment—sometimes even surgery, in severe cases—for infections from severe wounds. People with ED feel a sense of shame and embarrassment over their inability to control this behavior, which can lead to isolation and a decreased ability to function.

For an accurate diagnosis, it is important for clinicians to understand the difference between ED and nonsuicidal self-injury (NSSI). People with NSSI are motivated by constant, negative self-talk and feelings about themselves and the world around them, while people with ED are focused on fixing unwanted imperfections.

DIAGNOSTIC CONFUSION

Besides the possibility of confusing OCD with related disorders, the danger exists of confusing it with unrelated disorders that have similar symptoms.

Into the 1980s, the most frequent misdiagnosis for people with OCD was the psychotic disorder schizophrenia. People with psychotic disorders strongly believe illogical or bizarre thoughts. People with OCD, on the other hand, are plagued by doubt and generally realize that their obsessive thoughts are irrational. Another difference is that people with psychotic disorders often believe someone is inserting thoughts into their minds from outside, while people with OCD realize their obsessive thoughts are generated by their own minds.

Neuroscientist and OCD therapist Jim Hatton explained that the issue can become confused because some people with OCD, especially children, refer to their obsessive thoughts as voices. He said, "If you ask the person, 'Where does the voice come from? Is it inside your head or outside your head?' the person with OCD will say, 'It's inside,' and the person with a psychotic disorder will say, 'It's outside.'"[24]

Some people are misdiagnosed with ADHD because obsessive thoughts and mental rituals take up so much time that it seems as if they cannot pay attention. On the other hand, those with ADHD may be misdiagnosed with OCD. Because their difficulty in paying attention can result in mistakes, they may try to prevent this by counting or checking over and over in ways that look like OCD compulsions.

OCPD

Another unrelated disorder often confused with OCD is obsessive-compulsive personality disorder (OCPD), which involves an overall pattern of preoccupation with order and control. People with OCPD do not experience true obsessions and compulsions. Rather, they insist on everything being done according to rigid rules—such as keeping houses spotlessly clean or having possessions in a certain order—as part of their personal philosophy. They see no need to change their behavior and may, in fact, be proud

Both OCD and OCPD can cause conflict within families. This is why treatment is important.

of it. Treatment providers report that people with OCPD generally do not seek treatment unless forced to do so when threatened with losing their job, family, or friends.

Because OCPD and OCD have such similar names, many people mistakenly believe that they are the same disorder or that having one leads to developing the other. Hatton explained that not only are they two distinct disorders, but in some ways, they are completely opposite. "People with OCD hate the way they are and wish they could be like, quote, 'normal' people. People with OCPD think that they're right and everybody else ought to be like them. So it's a totally different thing. People with OCPD don't come into treatment. They think they're okay."[25]

Because OCD can be easily confused with other disorders, experts stress the need to seek a diagnosis from someone who is experienced with OCD and trained to distinguish it from other problems. Early diagnosis and treatment is beneficial because over time, the symptoms can become more deeply entrenched. Also, if OCD goes undiagnosed and untreated, other problems may develop that affect the person and their loved ones.

CHAPTER THREE

OCD'S EFFECTS

Religion can play a strong role in OCD. A woman named Diance gave one example: One day while she was in church, she glanced at a woman wearing a V-neck sweater, and out of nowhere, feelings of anxiety and shame overwhelmed her. From that moment, Diance was unable to look at anyone wearing even slightly revealing clothing because she was afraid she was sinning.

"'I was scared to look at people. I thought I was offending them by inappropriately glancing at them, and I constantly prayed for forgiveness,' said Diance, who stopped hugging family and friends and felt like a hypocrite in church."[26] Once an outgoing person, Diance stopped socializing with her friends, and if she did go to family events, she mostly slept through them. Desperate and too ashamed to tell anyone about what she was going through, she attempted suicide.

Diance was eventually diagnosed with scrupulosity, a type of OCD that is characterized by pervasive thoughts that someone is not religious or moral enough and that they are failing God in some way. Through therapy, Diance made tremendous strides in her recovery. "'Anxiety clouds your thinking,' [said] Diance, who started recording her thoughts as poetry and found a hidden passion for creative writing. 'Now when I read my poetry I can see how irrational my thinking was.'"[27]

Diance's story shows some of the effects of OCD,

Religion is comforting to many people, but it can also be a source of anxiety.

which can cause major problems at work, school, and home. OCD is a serious mental illness that should be taken seriously. For some people, it can even be life-threatening.

CAUSING PROBLEMS

OCD is a mental disorder, but the effects it has on a person's physical well-being and social and professional lives cannot be understated. A person with OCD often has a great deal of difficulty at their job. They may spend hours each morning on rituals and consistently fail to arrive at work on time. Those who check locks or stove knobs for hours before bedtime, then get up repeatedly during the night to check again, may find that their job performance falters due to lack of sleep. Some may lose their job; others may develop an obsession with the idea that they will lose their job and form new compulsions to deal with this fear.

Loss of employment can put a financial burden on people with OCD and their families. The nature of some compulsions also causes financial strain. Some people throw away large amounts of newly bought food or clothing because they believe it has become contaminated. Others spend an excessive amount of money on cleaning products.

Just as OCD can affect an adult's job performance, it can affect a student's school performance. Some students with OCD repeatedly check their answers or start rewriting an assignment over and over to make it "perfect." Their grades fall, not because they do not know the answers, but because they never finish tests or homework assignments despite spending a great deal of time on them.

Students with OCD may spend a long time packing their backpack the "right way."

OCD may also affect the ability to manage other responsibilities. Some are unable to care for their physical needs or household chores due to contamination fears or time spent on compulsions. They may become dependent on others to handle these matters.

FEELING ALONE

People with OCD may lose or fear losing relationships with people who are important to them. OCD can cause problems for families as well as friends, especially if the person with OCD demands that everyone in the household comply with their compulsions. They feel great anxiety if their demands are not met, while family members may be unwilling to remain in what

When OCD becomes severe enough to prevent people from leaving the house or socializing normally, a person can develop depression, which makes the situation feel worse.

they view as an intolerable situation. This is true for related disorders as well, such as hoarding disorder. Hatton said, "A lot of relationships fail because the hoarder can't let go of his stuff. I've seen people with hoarding make the choice of letting go of their marriage before they let go of their stuff."[28]

People with OCD may also lose relationships with people outside the home. Obsessive fears or time-consuming compulsions may keep them from socializing. Friends who do not understand the problem may withdraw. For example, one woman who developed an obsessive fear of being misunderstood repeatedly explained her actions in detail to her friends over the telephone, by letter, and in person. She said, "I lost a few friends over this. They could no longer put up with my explaining to them over and over and doubting their understanding. Some felt I questioned their intelligence."[29]

MORE THAN ONE DISORDER

People with OCD are at risk for having comorbid, or simultaneous, mental disorders. One of the most common of these is depression. Some research indicates that more than "60 percent of people with OCD have one major depressive episode at some point in their lives."[30]

People with OCD may become depressed for many reasons. They hate their symptoms but feel unable to control them. They may feel hopeless as important parts of their lives—relationships, jobs, and goals—suffer damage or slip away completely. They feel isolated when friends and loved ones fail to understand their disorder. Many suffer in silence, not confiding in others for fear of being misunderstood, especially if their intrusive thoughts are disgusting or frightening.

Although depression often results from OCD, some types of depression are caused by biological factors. Some people with OCD can also have biologically-based depression, just as they could also have other disorders not triggered by OCD.

Anxiety is another common disorder in people with OCD. Besides anxiety triggered by obsessions, people with OCD often feel a general sense of anxiety that causes them to worry excessively over everyday concerns. Anxiety causes physical symptoms such as rapid heartbeat, sweating, dizziness, and headaches. Some people develop phobias, suffer panic attacks, or fear leaving their homes.

Frustration over the effects of OCD can lead to anger or aggressive behavior. Penzel wrote, "This frustration can build up over time to high levels in some sufferers, particularly where their every goal in life is being ruined by the illness."[31]

Untreated OCD can lead to arguments.

Anger and frustration can also result when a time-consuming ritual fails to turn out the way it was intended or the ritual is interrupted. A person may become angry with family members who refuse to assist with compulsions, which can lead to conflict in the home.

It is estimated that substance abuse in people with OCD is close to 30 percent, which is almost twice as much as in the general population. They may self-medicate in an effort to make the irrational urges go away or to alleviate stress. The effect is temporary, and when the irrational urge returns, so does the urge to use substances, increasing the chance of dependency.

OCD AFFECTS EVERYONE

Because of the unique nature of its symptoms, OCD dominates many areas of family life. OCD therapist Barbara Van Noppe wrote, "Perhaps in no other psychological disorder is the family inexorably brought into the patient's illness than OCD."[32]

Family members often become depressed as they watch their loved one suffer. They may experience anxiety when something happens to set off the OCD symptoms. The stress can cause physical symptoms, such as headaches, gastrointestinal problems, and sleep problems. Like the person with OCD, family members sometimes try to cope through abuse of drugs or alcohol. Even when the family understands that their loved one cannot control the symptoms, they may feel anger and resentment for the ways the disorder has disrupted their lives.

Family members often struggle with guilt, suspecting that they are somehow to blame for their loved one's disorder. This is especially true of parents when a child is diagnosed with OCD.

Well-meaning people who fail to understand the disorder can make the situation worse. Psychology experts Gail Steketee and Nina A. Pruyn wrote, "Advice from friends and relatives may further reinforce the family's sense of guilt and shame as they are told that the patient is 'just going through a phase' or are given suggestions that more discipline or more attention is the solution to the patient's problem."[33]

FAMILY REACTIONS

The way family members react to their loved one's symptoms varies. At one extreme, they may oppose the symptoms, criticizing the person with OCD and demanding that they stop performing the compulsions. Since the person feels no control over the symptoms, this reaction only heightens their anxiety, which increases the OCD symptoms. They may start to perform their compulsions in secret, which increases their anxiety at the thought of being caught and scolded. At the other extreme are those family members who take part in OCD rituals, no matter how excessive or unreasonable, and take over household responsibilities and decisions that the person with OCD can no longer handle. Families are often divided between those hostile to the problem and those who believe they are protecting the person by indulging their symptoms. Psychiatrist Judith Rapoport noted that "OCD can distort family life, splitting it into warring factions and eliminating ordinary routine."[34]

Family members who participate in rituals do so in an effort to reduce their loved one's anxiety and keep peace in the household. Rapoport wrote about a mother who had been taking part in her son's excessive cleaning rituals. The mother said, "He had never been unreasonable before; he really was no different from most boys. So when he cared so much about something, even though I didn't understand it, I felt I had to go along. And he got so upset when I didn't."[35]

Steketee and Pruyn reported on the case of a young OCD patient who believed she needed to keep stacks of magazines on her parents' bed. She threw tantrums when her parents tried to move the magazines. "To keep the peace, they abandoned their bedroom to sleep in the living room on the couch."[36]

Despite their good intentions, family members who participate in OCD rituals help reinforce the problem. By indulging the compulsions and covering responsibilities, they enable the person with OCD to continue their rituals, perhaps even helping them function to the point where they see no need to seek treatment. Often, participating in rituals has the opposite effect of what the family members intend—it helps the disorder keep a firm grip on the person.

SEVERE CASES

Besides being unhealthy for the person with OCD, such a situation is also unhealthy for family members. In severe cases, OCD may control all areas of life and affect every decision the family makes. Steketee and Pruyn wrote:

> *Some families accommodate OCD symptoms to such an extent that their lifestyles revolve around the patient's requests. Many families become isolated, losing contact with extended family and friends outside of the home. Within the home, living situations can often become very restricted due to cleaning and washing rituals, fear of contamination, and hoarding that confines living space.*[37]

Some family members give up employment to care for their loved one. As a result, they not only experience financial strain but may also feel that they have lost a part of their identity. Some lose social contacts because it is difficult to invite people to the home or to go elsewhere. For example, a family member of one

Researching things such as medical symptoms is a common compulsion. A person may spend hours looking at various medical websites to try to be certain they do not have a particular illness.

person with OCD reported that the family had given up some social activities because OCD rituals made leaving the house a chore. The mother of another person with OCD reported that her son threw garbage on the bathroom floor because he feared touching the garbage can and that his room became filled with piles of clothes. His mother could not clean it up because he believed she made it more contaminated, and she stopped inviting people over because of the mess.

In the same way, hoarding often leads to social isolation for the family, who become embarrassed to allow anyone into the home. Experts compare the situation to the codependence found in families of alcoholics. The term "codependent" is used to describe someone who takes over the responsibilities of the person with OCD. They ignore their own needs and sacrifice parts of their own lives to cover for someone. As a result, neither person functions normally.

SUPPORT, NOT ENABLING

Instead of falling into such a trap, family members can take positive steps to help both their loved one

TIPS FOR FRIENDS AND FAMILY

The IOCDF created a list of guidelines for living with a loved one who has OCD. The guidelines should be tailored to each situation and may be more successful with the help of a therapist who has experience in working with people with OCD. The list includes tips such as:

- Watch for warning signals, such as repetitive behaviors, large amounts of unexplained alone time, continual lateness, and severe emotional reactions.
- Change expectations—someone with OCD is going to have many ups and downs, and recovery does not always go smoothly.
- Remember that treatment is not the same for everyone—some people take longer to overcome OCD than others.
- Avoid daily comparisons of the person's behavior.
- Recognize every victory, no matter how small.
- Create a supportive atmosphere.
- Set limits when appropriate, depending on the person's mood.
- Make sure the person is taking any necessary medication.
- Communicate clearly and concisely.
- Others in the household should each make time for themselves.
- Do not let OCD take over the household—it is okay to have a conversation about something else.
- Keep routines as normal as possible.
- Do not accommodate or participate in the rituals.
- Create goals as a family.

and themselves. The first step is accepting that their loved one has OCD. Some families react with denial, but if they fail to acknowledge the problem, they are unable to help and may even hinder the person with OCD from getting proper treatment.

Family and friends can also learn more about OCD. Understanding the nature of the disorder will allow them to be supportive and encouraging. It will also help them avoid hurtful remarks and attitudes based on misconceptions, such as telling the person with OCD that they could stop their compulsions if they really wanted to do so. It is also helpful to make a distinction between the person and the disorder, remembering that OCD is only a part of their loved one, not the whole person.

Since OCD often takes over the lives of family members, experts recommend that family members give enough attention to their own needs. If they fail to care for themselves, they will be in no position to help the person with OCD. Rather than continuing to cover for their loved one, family members should require them to handle their own responsibilities as they are able.

To help their loved one recover, family members must stop taking part in OCD rituals. Simply stopping all at once could cause the person with OCD distress that would increase their symptoms, especially if the family has been participating in rituals for a long time. Rather, experts recommend developing a plan to lessen participation over time. If possible, this should be done with the help of an OCD therapist. When refusing to take part in rituals, family members should be kind but firm. If a person with OCD becomes angry or upset because a friend or family member does not continue to perform such behavior as answering repeated questions, the loved one can remind them that taking part in the ritual will reinforce the OCD and possibly even make it worse.

At times, the family's refusal to take part in rituals and insistence that the person care for their own responsibilities may motivate them to seek treatment if they were previously unwilling to do so. The decision to seek professional help can make all the difference, since effective treatments exist for OCD.

TREATMENT OPTIONS

Researchers do not know for sure what causes OCD. There are many theories, but it is most likely that OCD is caused by a combination of several components, including biology, genetics, and environment. There are also additional risk factors that can trigger OCD; for instance, someone who has experienced a traumatic event such as abuse or the death of a parent will have an increased chance of developing OCD symptoms, especially if OCD runs in the family.

PASSED DOWN FROM PARENTS

Researchers are examining the question of whether or not OCD could be inherited. They have not yet identified a specific gene that causes OCD, but studies of patterns in families support the idea of a genetic basis. An estimated 2 to 3 percent of the general population experiences OCD at some time during their lives, but rates among family members of people with OCD are much higher. A study published in the *Journal of the American Academy of Child and Adolescent Psychiatry* showed that 30 percent of the children in the study affected by OCD had either a parent or sibling with OCD.

Several studies have focused on twins. In 47 to 50 percent of cases of fraternal, or non-identical, twins where one twin had OCD, the other also had it. In 80 to 87 percent of OCD cases involving identical twins, both twins had OCD. Twin studies have also shown that genetics are more likely to be a factor when OCD is diagnosed before the age of 18 (45 to 65 percent), compared to those who were diagnosed as adults (27 to 47 percent).

Twin studies have found that genetic makeup does play a role in the development of OCD, but it is not the only factor.

Researchers have examined the question of whether OCD is truly inherited or if it is a learned behavior that people develop from exposure to relatives who have the disorder. Family studies have shown that relatives with OCD often have very different symptoms. This suggests that it is not a learned behavior but likely has a genetic basis.

If OCD is linked with a particular gene or genes, this does not mean that a person who inherits the gene will automatically develop OCD. Rather, researchers believe the presence of such a gene could predispose a person to OCD. In other words, if the person is exposed to a trigger such as high stress or a traumatic event, the presence of the gene could make it more likely that OCD will develop. This may be one reason that one-third to two-thirds of people with OCD report that their symptoms began at the same time that they experienced a stressful or life-changing event, such as giving birth or dealing with the death of a family member. Other people, however, report experiencing no such triggering event before dvelop-ing OCD symptoms.

Another suggestion is that in order for people to develop OCD, they have to inherit a combination of genes. Some of these genes act as modifiers

THE ROLE OF THE BRAIN

While it is not known exactly what causes OCD, research suggests parts of the brain may play a role in the disorder. These parts include:

- **basal ganglia:** triggers and controls voluntary movement. Studies have shown that damage to the basal ganglia may sometimes cause OCD symptoms.
- **orbitofrontal cortex (OFC):** organizes and interprets information.
- **anterior cingulate gyrus (ACG):** plays a part in autonomic functions as well as emotional behavior, decision making, and impulse control. The OFC and ACG communicate with the basal ganglia and are responsible for finding "mistakes" in brain circuits. In people with OCD, these areas of the brain are more active. When overexcited, they cannot detect the mistakes, so they alert the basal ganglia that there is a problem when nothing is wrong. The brain becomes stuck in this hyperactive mode and begins firing off intrusive thoughts.
- **caudate nucleus:** component of the basal ganglia; helps regulate thoughts and voluntary movement by separating important information that needs to be acted upon from unimportant information. It is believed the hyper-excitement may be caused by a faulty caudate nucleus.
- **thalamus:** receives and transmits messages from one brain area to another. Overproduction by the thalamus floods the frontal lobe, which increases OCD symptoms and hyperactivity in an endless cycle.

to turn on the gene or genes associated with OCD. This is one possible reason why a healthy person could later develop OCD without being exposed to a stressful event.

TOO MUCH BRAIN ACTIVITY

Researchers believe certain brain areas are involved in the development of OCD. One prominent theory is that OCD symptoms arise in a circuit of nerve pathways between the basal ganglia and a part of the

- **serotonin:** a neurotransmitter, or chemical messenger, that delivers nerve impulses between these areas. People with OCD may have too little serotonin in their brain.

PARTS OF THE BRAIN

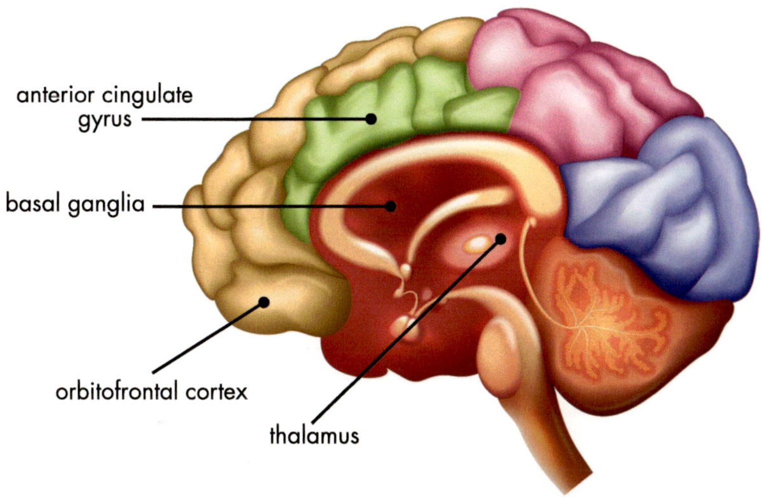

The brain is a complicated organ, and many different parts play a role in mental illnesses such as OCD.

frontal lobes called the orbitofrontal cortex. A component of the basal ganglia called the caudate nucleus is believed to play a role as well.

Every second, the brain receives a flood of information about important and unimportant matters. One responsibility of the caudate nucleus is to separate unimportant information from important information that needs to be acted upon. Evidence shows that the caudate nucleus in some people with OCD is overactive. Hatton explained:

> *This part of the brain can be thought of as acting like a gate, or a filtering mechanism, separating out the things you need to pay attention to from those you don't. With this part of the mechanism over-active, it's as if the gate has been stuck open, and nothing can be kept out. So, people with OCD are likely to be both over-stimulated and have a reduced ability to filter out irrelevant information.*[38]

The overactive caudate nucleus sends this unfiltered information along to the thalamus, which in turn sends it to the orbitofrontal cortex. The orbitofrontal cortex then interprets and triggers a response to information that normally would have been ignored.

LOOKING AT THE BRAIN

Evidence from brain imaging studies supports the idea that these brain regions are involved in OCD. Some imaging studies have examined brain structure, while others have examined brain function.

To view brain structure, researchers use computerized axial tomography (CAT) scans, which involve taking many different X-rays to form a cross-sectional or three-dimensional image. They also use magnetic resonance imaging (MRI) scans, which use a magnetic field and sound waves to create a computerized image of the brain. Five out of twelve studies conducted in these ways showed no differences between the brain structure of OCD patients and that of non-sufferers. The other seven studies found differences, especially in the caudate nucleus and the frontal lobes. These differences varied from study to study. To sum up the evidence gathered from these types of studies, Gail Steketee and Teresa Pigott wrote, "Although these findings are inconsistent and not particularly impressive, they suggest that structural brain abnormalities may not be uncommon in OCD."[39]

Researchers have found greater evidence of the role of certain brain areas in OCD by using imaging studies that examine brain function. Functional MRI (fMRI) produces a quick succession of images that can be compared to show changes in brain activity. In positron emission tomography (PET) and single photon emission computerized tomography (SPECT), a radioactive substance is injected into the body, and the radiation it emits is translated into a computerized image. These scans have revealed that, compared to people without the disorder, most people with OCD had increased activity in the caudate nucleus of the basal ganglia. During some imaging studies, people with OCD were exposed to their fears, either directly or by imagining the feared situation. When this happened, they showed higher than normal activity in the orbitofrontal cortex and basal ganglia.

Some scans showed higher than normal activity in one part of the basal ganglia known as the amygdala. Part of the amygdala's job is signaling fear. Hatton explained, "This suggests that people with OCD are living in a state of heightened fear all the time. This might mean that people with OCD are more sensitive to fearful subjects, although we actually observe in practice that while someone might be horrified by their obsessions, a very scary movie might not faze them at all."[40]

USING BRAIN SCANS IN TREATMENT

Cognitive behavioral therapy (CBT) is a common course of therapy for people with OCD, but it does not work with everyone. CBT is a widely practiced course of therapy in which patients learn to separate themselves from the intrusive thoughts. Part of this therapy also involves patient exposure to their fears. This therapy is supposed to help patients gradually learn how to better deal with their anxieties. Dr. Jamie Feusner and Joseph O'Neill, associate professors at UCLA Semel Institute, wanted to see if using brain scans would tell them which patients would benefit from CBT.

The team used MRI imaging to examine the brains of 17 people, ages 21 to 50, with OCD. Their brains were scanned before and after receiving CBT. What they found was that CBT does increase connections in certain areas of the brain, which likely means more effective brain activity. They also discovered that people who had better brain connectivity before the treatment had much worse connectivity afterwards.

While this study was not conclusive in determining who would benefit long-term from CBT, it was a breakthrough because it was the first time brain scans were used in this way. Dr. Emily Stern, associate professor of psychiatry and neuroscience at the Mount Sinai School of Medicine in New York City, said that a brain scan that has potential "to predict which patients will relapse has the potential to identify those patients who may need further treatment or greater monitoring."[1]

1. Quoted in Mary Elizabeth Dallas, "Could Brain Scans Help Guide Treatment for OCD?," WebMD, June 26, 2015. www.webmd.com/mental-health/news/20150626/could-brain-scans-help-guide-treatment-for-ocd#3.

AN UNUSUAL LINK

Some researchers are studying the possibility that other illnesses that affect the basal ganglia are linked to the onset of OCD symptoms. An infection commonly called strep throat, which is caused by *Streptococcus* bacteria, afflicts people who are mainly between the ages of 5 and 15. If left untreated, strep throat can lead to rheumatic fever and inflammation that can affect the heart, brain, joints, and skin. Up to 10 percent of people who get rheumatic fever go on to develop Sydenham's chorea, a disorder that results in uncontrollable jerking movements that generally go away after a few weeks or months. Doctors believe Sydenham's chorea develops because antibodies that the immune system develops to fight the infection mistakenly target and destroy cells in the basal ganglia. When the immune system misidentifies and attacks body cells, this is called an autoimmune response.

In rare cases, the bacteria that causes strep throat can also trigger OCD.

In the late 1980s, doctors observed that a large percentage of people with Sydenham's chorea developed OCD symptoms. This observation led to further research about a possible connection between strep throat and OCD. Researchers discovered that some children with OCD suddenly developed their symptoms after a strep throat infection. They believe this likely happens because of the same type of autoimmune response found with Sydenham's chorea, in which antibodies attack nerve cells in the basal ganglia. This condition is called pediatric autoimmune neuropsychiatric disorders associated with streptococcal infections (PANDAS). In MRI scans, children with PANDAS showed enlarged basal ganglia compared with other children.

PANDAS accounts for only a small percentage of children who have OCD symptoms. In contrast with typical OCD patients, who may develop symptoms gradually, children with PANDAS suddenly develop strong OCD symptoms. Their parents can often pinpoint the exact day when symptoms began. When these children are treated with antibiotics, their OCD symptoms lessen, but if a strep infection occurs again, the OCD symptoms worsen. Some children with PANDAS have also been treated with plasmapheresis, a procedure that filters antibodies from the blood.

BRAIN CHEMICALS

Chemicals in the brain called neurotransmitters help relay messages between different parts of the brain. One way the brain regions that appear to be involved in OCD communicate with each other is through a neurotransmitter called serotonin.

Serotonin assists in relaying messages between different areas of the brain. It does this by helping electrical impulses travel from one neuron to the next. Serotonin is stored in neurons inside tiny sacs called vesicles. When an electrical impulse travels along a neuron, the neuron's vesicles release serotonin. The serotonin crosses the synapse, or gap, between the first neuron and the next. The serotonin then fits into receptors on the receiving neuron. Serotonin in a receptor works like a key fitting into a lock. It opens up a channel that allows the electrical impulse from the first neuron to move across the synapse and flow through the receiving neuron. Once the electrical message has been delivered, the vesicles take the serotonin back. The return of the serotonin to the first neuron is called "reuptake."

The theory about the role of serotonin in OCD is that reuptake occurs before the electrical impulse has a chance to travel to the receiving neuron. As a result, the communication circuits between the frontal lobes and the basal ganglia fail to function properly.

The greatest evidence supporting this theory involves a group of drugs commonly used to treat depression. These drugs are called selective serotonin reuptake inhibitors (SSRIs) because they prevent serotonin from being taken back into the vesicles before they deliver their message. The effect of SSRIs on OCD was discovered in the 1960s. Patients who had both depression and OCD were given an SSRI to treat the depression. After treatment with the drug, their OCD symptoms also lessened. Drugs that affect other neurotransmitters do not have this effect.

Further evidence comes from imaging studies that examine brain function. People with OCD who showed higher than normal activity in their frontal lobes or basal ganglia on brain scans were rescanned after they had been treated with SSRIs. In patients

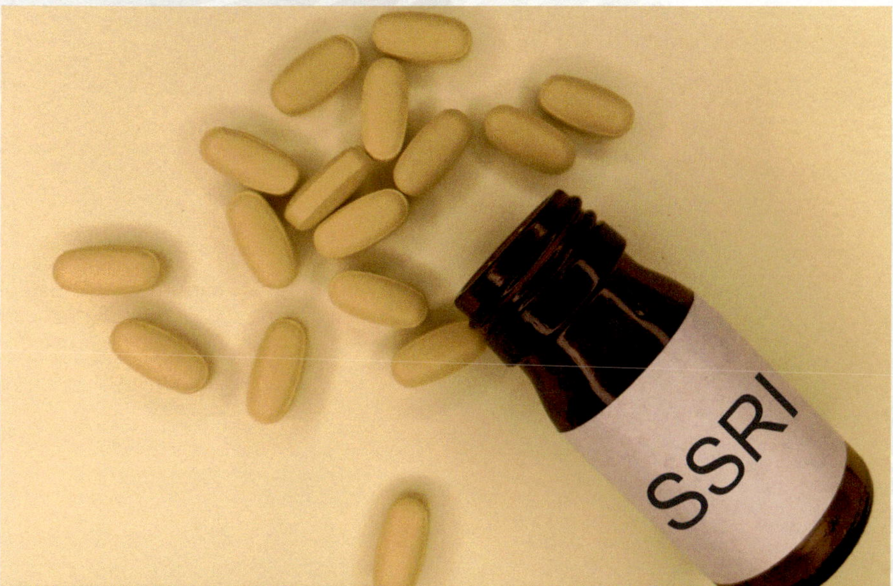

SSRIs such as Prozac and Zoloft have had great success in treating OCD. Because they work so well for so many people, they are often considered an important part of treatment.

whose OCD symptoms had lessened with SSRI treatment, the scans also showed that the abnormal brain activity had been reversed. This did not occur for patients whose OCD symptoms had not responded to SSRIs.

THE ROLE OF MEDICATION

SSRIs play a large role in the medical treatment of OCD. In fact, the only five medications approved by the U.S. Food and Drug Administration (FDA) for treating OCD are all SSRIs. They are fluvoxamine (Luvox), fluoxetine (Prozac), clomipramine (Anafranil), sertraline (Zoloft), and paroxetine (Paxil).

Of the five drugs, Anafranil carries the greatest risk of side effects. This is because it not only affects serotonin but also other brain chemicals. Its side effects include dizziness, fatigue, increased heart rate, weight gain, and constipation. An overdose of Anafranil can trigger seizures, cause abnormal heart rhythms, and even be fatal. For these reasons, doctors often prefer trying other medications first, especially when patients have another medical condition involving seizures or heart problems.

Side effects for the other four generally include nausea, headaches, fatigue, and nervousness. In rare cases, suicidal thoughts can be a side effect, and someone who experiences such thoughts should talk to their doctor right away. Often, the side effects stop after the patient has used the drugs for a few weeks, but they can start again if the person stops taking their medication too suddenly.

Even though these medications are the only drugs approved by the FDA specifically to treat OCD, they are not the only drugs that doctors use for this. The FDA has approved other drugs for other mental disorders, and since these drugs work much like the approved medications, doctors also prescribe these for

OCD. These include citalopram (Celexa), escitalopram (Lexapro), and duloxatine (Cymbalta). When an OCD patient does not show significant improvement after trying several different SSRIs, treatment providers often add another type of medication to be taken along with an SSRI.

When strategies involving SSRIs fail, treatment providers may try a different type of drug. Studies of other types of antidepressants, such as venlafaxine (Effexor), and antianxiety drugs, such as buspirone (BuSpar) and clonazepam (Klonopin), suggest that these are sometimes successful in treating OCD. A class of antidepressants called monoamine oxidase inhibitors (MAOIs) may help some people with OCD, especially those who also suffer from panic disorder. Because MAOIs interact with certain foods and drugs to produce dangerous—and possibly lethal—side effects, patients must follow a strict diet when taking them as well as for a few weeks after stopping their use. Steketee and Pigott wrote, "MAOI use for patients with OCD should likely be restricted to those who fail to respond to [SSRIs] and have access to a clinician experienced in dealing with MAOI treatment issues."[41]

LOOKING FOR OTHER FACTORS

Before concluding that a drug has failed, patients and treatment providers should consider other factors. One reason why a drug may appear ineffective could be that the patient did not take it long enough to produce results. It sometimes takes up to 12 weeks for some medications to produce the desired effect. Another common reason is that the dosage was incorrect. To be effective for treating OCD, SSRIs generally have to be taken in higher doses than when used for treating depression. In some cases, beginning with a high dose causes strong side effects that can lead

Any new medication should be discussed with a doctor to make sure the patient does not have any health conditions or other medications that could interact poorly with the new prescription.

the patient to stop taking the drug. Beginning with a lower dose and raising it as necessary may prevent this and lead to successful treatment.

Another factor leading to the failure of medical treatment for OCD could be unrealistic expectations. Teresa Pigott and Sheila Seay wrote, "Some patients with OCD, and some clinicians, do not know, or cannot accept, that partial symptom reduction is the usual 'response' in OCD. As a result, they can be erroneously designated 'treatment failures,' when they are in fact experiencing a level of symptom reduction that is 'average.'"[42] In other words, SSRIs do not cure OCD; they only lessen the symptoms. Someone whose medication is helping them may go long stretches of time without OCD symptoms, only to encounter an intense trigger and experience a flare-up, or sudden return of the symptoms they had before the medication started working. Such flare-ups are not uncommon for people with OCD, but they can cause distress if the patient is unaware of this. The person with OCD may worry that their medication is no longer working or that their OCD has gotten worse. In reality, once the trigger has been dealt with, the symptoms typically subside again.

TMS FOR OCD

In addition to medication, a treatment called transcranial magnetic stimulation (TMS) has been approved by the FDA to treat OCD that is especially resistant to therapy and medication. In this type of treatment, an electromagnetic coil is placed on a person's scalp. The strong magnet changes the chemistry of the patient's brain in a way that reduces OCD symptoms. TMS has shown great results in reducing depression that is resistant to other forms of treatment, and now it is showing the same success with treatment-resistant OCD. According to the IOCDF, between 45 and 55 percent of patients who underwent TMS experienced reduced OCD symptoms for about a month after each session.

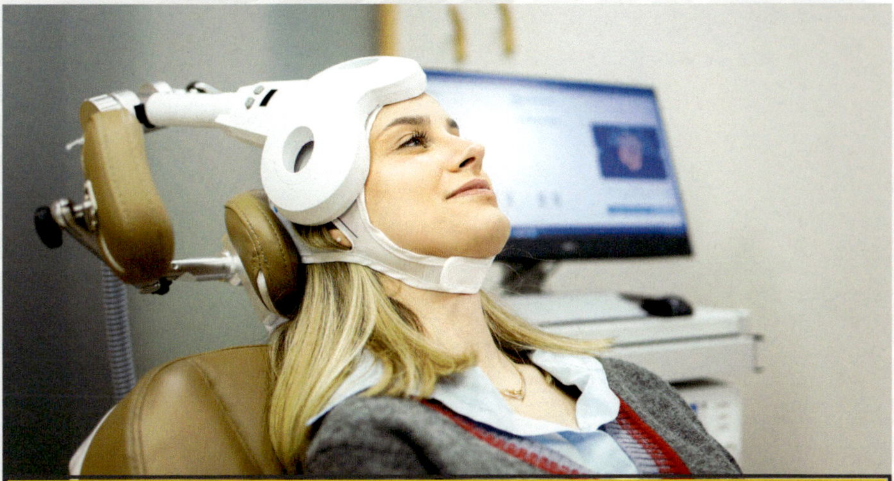

TMS is a safe and effective treatment for depression and OCD. As it has become more widely available over the years, it is now recommended more often.

OCD THERAPIES

Therapy is also an important part of OCD treatment. Just like there are a variety of medications for OCD, there are a variety of therapies. What works best for some people may not work well for others. However, according to the IOCDF, therapy combined with medication benefits nearly 70 percent of people with OCD.

Therapy has a long history, but finding the right type of therapy to treat OCD has been challenging. One of the earliest types of therapy was called psychoanalytic treatment. It was developed by Austrian neurologist Sigmund Freud, and it was is based on the belief that current psychological problems are caused by earlier experiences in life, such as childhood traumas or parenting methods. The treatment provider tries to bring patients relief by helping them identify and face underlying problems in their past.

In his 1909 case of Ernst Lanzer, called the "Rat Man" case, Freud used this method to treat a patient suffering from obsessive thoughts about rats. Freud's writings about his success in treating this patient led other doctors to adopt his methods. However, the patient died in World War I (1914-1918), making it impossible to see if the treatment would bring him long-term relief.

Psychoanalysis remained the standard treatment for OCD into the 1970s, but it proved to be mostly ineffective, even for mild cases. At that time, there was a growing body of evidence that pointed to biological factors in OCD, such as abnormal function of certain brain areas. Freud's theories were later largely discredited, and few people practice psychoanalysis today.

Sometimes past trauma is at the root of OCD. A therapist can help OCD sufferers address their trauma so their OCD symptoms lessen.

CBT

At the same time that Freud was studying OCD, French psychologist and neurologist Pierre Janet reported success in treating compulsions with techniques aimed at modifying present behavior. Freud's writings about the Rat Man case shifted attention away from behavioral techniques, but in the 1950s, researchers again began experimenting with behavioral therapies to treat OCD.

The theory behind different types of behavioral therapies is that obsessions develop when the person comes to associate a neutral object or situation with anxiety. For example, they may associate a garbage can with the fear of contamination. In an effort to cope with the anxiety, the person develops escape and avoidance behaviors in the form of compulsions; in this case, not going near a trash can.

Cognitive behavioral therapy (CBT) was invented in the 1960s by psychiatrist Aaron Beck. He observed that during his psychotherapy sessions, some patients seemed to have an internal dialogue going on in their minds. However, they did not always verbalize

UNHELPFUL PHRASES

OCD is not like what may be depicted in movies in TV shows. It is not just needing to carry around a bottle of hand sanitizer or have an organized room. In an opinion article for the British publication *Metro*, OCD patient Hattie Gladwell said, "When people who haven't been diagnosed with obsessive compulsive disorder describe their ways as being 'seriously OCD' it almost feels like some of the severity of the illness is taken away and people see it in a lighter way than they should."[1] OCD is a debilitating illness that is different for each person with the disorder. The unique nature of the disorder can create misunderstandings, leading some people to say things that are unintentionally hurtful. When someone hears the same comments multiple times, it can become frustrating for them and make an already stressful situation worse. Gladwell provided a list of comments that can deeply hurt someone who has been diagnosed with the disorder:

- *"Oh don't worry, I do that too sometimes"* …
- *"So why is your room a mess?"* …
- *"I am being so OCD today!"* …
- *"I love my OCD!"* …
- *"Can you just stop that?"* …
- *"It's all in your head"* …
- *"You're over-exaggerating"* …
- *"You should come over and clean my house!"* …
- *"You don't look like you have OCD"* …
- *"Just relax"* …
- *"Other people have it worse!"*[2]

1. Hattie Gladwell, "12 Things you Shouldn't Say to Someone with OCD," *Metro*, December 17, 2015. metro.co.uk/2015/12/17/12-things-you-shouldnt-say-to-someone-with-ocd-5571877/.

2. Gladwell, "12 Things you Shouldn't Say to Someone with OCD."

those thoughts. For example, during a session, the client might be thinking to themselves: "'He (the therapist) hasn't said much today. I wonder if he's annoyed with me?' These thoughts might make the client feel slightly anxious or perhaps annoyed. He or she could then respond to this thought with a further thought: 'He's probably tired, or perhaps I haven't been talking about the most important things.' The second thought might change how the client was feeling."[43]

Beck used the term "automatic thoughts" to describe such thoughts that enter the person's head. These are different than impulsive or intrusive thoughts because they are not connected to any kind of action, either wanted or unwanted. They are thoughts that pass through a person's mind and often have an impact on emotions. Beck thought that the patient's ability to identify and report automatic thoughts was the key to improving their mental health. A person who can challenge their negative thoughts and replace them with positive thoughts is more likely to experience positive mood changes as well.

CBT is widely practiced for many different kinds of mental disorders, including OCD, depression, and anxiety. In CBT, the patient learns to separate themselves from their intrusive thoughts and to understand that they have no basis in reality. Obsessions are challenged with rational alternatives and behavioral techniques are learned to change compulsive behavior. When this type of therapy is successful, the patient eventually realizes that the obsession is unimportant, which reduces the intrusive thoughts. However, this type of CBT, which is sometimes called "talk therapy," is not the most effective treatment for OCD because most OCD sufferers already realize that their intrusive thoughts are irrational.

Because OCD causes intense doubt, arguing with themselves tends to be useless for a sufferer, as their mind keeps coming up with new reasons why the obsession is important. For example, someone might have an intrusive thought that their best friend does not like them anymore and no longer wants to maintain a friendship. If the person thinks, 'That's silly. I didn't do anything to upset her between last week and this week, so it's illogical to think that she just decided not to be friends with me anymore,' their OCD will likely come up with dozens of reasons why this line of reasoning is incorrect. For example, the person might later think, 'She said she was ok with me canceling plans on Wednesday, but maybe she was lying.' Eventually, to get relief from these thoughts, they will perform a compulsion. This can be anything from calling the friend to ask for reassurance, ruminating about what evidence there is that their friend is or is not mad at them, or even seeking out a psychic to try to find out what their friend is thinking.

ERP

The most important type of therapy for people with OCD is exposure and response prevention (ERP). To prepare for ERP, the patient and treatment provider work together to identify the patient's obsessions and compulsions. They then create a list of various situations in which the symptoms cause anxiety. Each item on the list may include both an exposure to a fear and a response prevention, such as touching a dirty doorknob and not washing afterward.

The treatment provider next asks the patient to rate each item on the Subjective Units of Distress Scale (SUDS). The patient gives each item a score of 0 to 100 to show how much anxiety each would provoke. The items are then put into a hierarchy, from least to most anxiety-provoking.

ERP generally begins with an item that the patient has rated as moderately anxiety-provoking. The patient is then exposed to the feared situation and asked to resist the urge to perform the compulsive rituals that have been their way of dealing with the anxiety. The exposure continues until the anxiety lessens.

Ideally, it should be repeated daily until the situation no longer creates anxiety, even at the beginning of the exposure.

REAL OR IMAGINED

The exposures involved in ERP can be either acted out in real life (a process called "in vivo exposure") or imagined. With in vivo exposure, a person with contamination obsessions might be asked to touch or handle something they think of as dirty. A person with obsessive fears regarding a certain number might be asked to perform an action that number of times. The treatment provider sometimes uses a technique called modeling, in which they first perform the action to

Treatment for people with contamination OCD may involve things such as asking them to touch a bathroom door handle without using a tissue as a germ barrier.

ERP has been shown to be the most effective type of therapy for OCD, but it typically increases a person's anxiety before decreasing it. For this reason, ERP can feel scary to an OCD sufferer.

demonstrate what the patient needs to do. Some sessions take place in the treatment provider's office. At other times, the treatment provider accompanies the patient into situations that trigger fear. For example, they might go to a place that the patient fears is contaminated, such as a hospital waiting room.

When a feared situation is difficult or impossible to present in vivo, such as when the obsession involves hurting themselves or others, imagined exposure is used. The treatment provider describes a scene about a feared situation, including sensory details to make the scene as real as possible. The patient pictures themselves in the scene as if it is happening. This continues until their anxiety decreases.

TOLERATING UNCERTAINTY

To be effective, the exposure to the feared situation must last long enough for the patient to feel their anxiety decrease significantly. Although the initial exposure—such as touching a doorknob—might be brief, the response prevention—not washing hands—continues until the patient no longer needs to do it.

RANKING FEARS

An exposure hierarchy is a list therapists use to document the sources of a person's anxiety by the level of fear they experience when faced with the source. A SUDS scale is used to measure the anxiety—from 0, which is completely relaxed, to 100, which is the worst anxiety imaginable.

Here is an example of what a hierarchy might look like in a person with fear of contamination:

1. *Putting hand in toilet bowl water (SUDS rating: 100)*
2. *Touching toilet seat (SUDS rating: 95)*
3. *Touching floor beside toilet (SUDS rating: 90)*
4. *Handling raw poultry or hamburger meat (SUDS rating: 85)*
5. *Touching wall in [bathroom] (SUDS rating: 80)*
6. *Touching bathroom door handle (SUDS rating: 75)*
7. *Shaking hands with a stranger (SUDS rating: 65)*
8. *Touching the bottom of your shoe (SUDS rating: 60)*
9. *Pressing a button on a vending machine (SUDS rating: 55)*
10. *Handling money (SUDS rating: 50)*[1]

1. Owen Kelly, PhD, "What Is an Exposure Hierarchy? An Essential Piece of Exposure Therapy," *VeryWell*, March 14, 2017. www.verywell.com/what-is-an-exposure-hierarchy-2510646.

The main goal of ERP is to make the patient better able to tolerate uncertainty. OCD is the search for 100 percent certainty that nothing bad will happen. By exposing themselves to their fear and not taking any action to prevent it, the person gradually rewires their brain to realize that action is not needed in all cases of uncertainty, and that uncertainty does not automatically indicate danger.

Each fear successfully overcome makes the next in the hierarchy easier to deal with. Hatton explained:

> *As opposed to climbing a ladder where the higher up the ladder you go the farther off the ground you feel, this is more like having a stack of lumber in your front yard, and as you're kicking out the bottom boards, the stack is getting shorter. So things at the top of your hierarchy come down in value as you're working on the bottom thing.*[44]

As a result, items at the top of the hierarchy that once seemed impossible for the patient to face now become manageable.

The number of therapy sessions needed with the treatment provider varies from patient to patient. Once patients have completed the ERP phase of the therapy, they need to continue practicing ERP to maintain what they have accomplished. This is because OCD is never cured; it is managed, and the symptoms could flare up again. A maintenance program could include occasional follow-up sessions with the treatment provider, in person or by telephone, and even at-home exposure therapy. Hatton explained the importance of this:

> *You can't just sit there, with your hands up in the air for an hour after touching a contaminated object and wait it out. You have to go on with the rest of your life. If you just sit there, not only will it take up an hour of your precious time, but you will also [spread] in your mind the idea that your hands are really contaminated. So go about whatever you were doing as if you hadn't experienced any anxiety. Eventually you will be able to separate the anxiety from the exposure; your brain will learn that they are two separate things and that you do not have to do the ritual in order for the anxiety to come back down by itself.*[45]

A DIFFICULT TASK

ERP takes a great deal of effort on the part of the patient. Penzel wrote, "I tell everybody when they come to see me that all I have to offer them is hard work, but that if they do it, they'll get better."[46]

Studies testify to the good results of following through on a program of ERP. Some studies showed that 85 percent of patients who completed ERP experienced moderate to complete improvement in their OCD symptoms. However, because ERP is difficult and stressful, over 25 percent of people with OCD either refuse ERP therapy or fail to complete it. Hatton explained, "Exposure means facing your fears, and response prevention means not doing your safety maneuver. So when you describe it that way, it sounds like somebody's worst nightmare."[47]

ERP only works if it is done consistently. Patients must make sure to schedule regular appointments.

Tolerating uncertainty can be easier said than done. When someone has been stuck in an obsession for hours, they sometimes give in and perform their compulsion to get some relief. The person may then feel that they are a failure. In some cases, they may take it as proof that ERP is not helping them and quit therapy altogether. However, it is important for patients to remember that overcoming a mental illness is not a straightforward or easy process. There will be days when they simply cannot tolerate the distress, and other days where facing their fears takes almost no effort at all. The most important thing is to keep trying even when it feels hard.

CHAPTER FIVE

LIVING WITH OCD

While treatment is necessary to help a person with OCD live well and successfully manage their disorder, they often face barriers, include limited health insurance options and the cost of treatment. In the past, finding therapists who were experienced in treating OCD could also be a challenge. However, thanks to both growing awareness of OCD and the increasing availability of telehealth, or therapy sessions conducted by video over the internet, this barrier has been steadily decreasing in recent years. OCD advocates hope other barriers will be similarly dismantled in the future.

FINDING A GROUP

One treatment option that can help people both get therapy for their OCD and meet other people who have experienced similar difficulties is called group therapy. In this type of therapy, several different patients meet at the same time with the treatment provider.

Group therapy can be very beneficial in treating OCD. People with OCD may feel isolated and embarrassed by their symptoms. These feelings sometimes decrease once they see that others in the group are facing the same challenges. They learn by observing how others are dealing with similar symptoms. Members of the group often feel an increased sense of self-worth as they are able to help each other with suggestions and encouragement. The warm, understanding atmosphere is refreshing for people with a disorder that is often misunderstood. Making new friends can also be helpful, since a strong support system is crucial in managing any mental illness.

Even when loved ones are well-meaning, they often struggle to understand how OCD affects someone, which means their advice is not always helpful. Group therapy can help people find support from others who know what living with OCD is like.

Group therapy can provide a way for people to connect with others they enjoy spending time with. The benefit of having other friends with OCD is that they can all help each other outside of therapy as well. They can point out when their friend is having irrational thoughts, as opposed to when something is a genuine danger that should be addressed. This can be difficult for a person with OCD to distinguish on their own because they are so used to everything feeling like a serious emergency. Once someone has realized they are experiencing intrusive thoughts, they are better able to put their ERP training into practice.

For someone to get the most benefits from group therapy, it is important that they fully participate in each session as well as attend each one. It may be tempting to sit back and let others talk during the sessions, but sharing one's own experiences allows the individual to work through their situation.

FAMILY THERAPY

Some therapy groups include family members of the OCD patients. This helps family members better understand the nature of their loved one's disorder. Hatton pointed out another benefit:

> *Learning that you (and they) are not alone, and that others have had experiences and anxieties very similar to yours, can be very reassuring and validating. This is true whether you are one of the OCD sufferers, or a family member of someone with OCD whose family experiences are necessarily different in some ways from those of people whose family dynamics do not include OCD.*[48]

Again, this is an important part of building up a strong support network. When family members understand what OCD is and how to successfully combat it, the lives of everyone in the family improves. Family members' attendance at ERP sessions can be

Family therapy can be helpful, especially when a child or teen is diagnosed with OCD.

COMMON OCD THEMES

The thoughts of people with OCD generally follow certain themes. For example, a person who has harm OCD often thinks about the possibility that they will hurt someone else. Harm OCD intrusive thoughts can include fears about leaving the stove on and burning down the house, tripping while holding a knife, or punching someone for no reason.

Health OCD typically involves intrusive concerns about things such as whether a spot on the skin is a freckle or a sign of cancer or whether a mild sickness will turn deadly. If someone has both harm and health OCD, they may worry that if they cough around someone else, they will pass on some disease they are unaware they have.

Relationship OCD involves fears about a romantic partner, friends, or family members. Someone with this theme may have intrusive worries that they do not actually love their partner, that their marriage will break up without warning, or that their friends secretly wish they would go away.

These are only a few common OCD themes. Some people have multiple themes—sometimes at the same exact time—while others deal with only one.

helpful when it comes to the patient completing homework assignments. Family members who understand ERP and who know what their loved one is trying to accomplish between sessions are in a better position to give needed support and encouragement. They also may need support themselves to stop accommodating behaviors.

Family therapy can also help in situations where the OCD symptoms have caused conflict or communication problems within the family. The treatment provider can help all involved to develop better communication and problem-solving skills.

ALTERNATIVE TREATMENTS

Besides seeking out ways to apply behavior therapy, some people have tried alternative treatments for OCD, such as hypnosis, relaxation training, and eye movement desensitization and reprocessing (EMDR). Occasionally, a person with OCD will report that such a treatment brought relief. This may be because such treatments can affect an underlying cause of OCD. For example, EMDR has been shown to be most effective for helping people overcome past trauma. If someone has developed OCD in response to trauma, EMDR may be very helpful to them, while not being helpful at all to someone whose OCD is the result of a chemical imbalance in the brain. Sometimes it takes trial and error for a person to find the combination of treatments that work best for them.

The Natural Standard Research Collaboration provided a list of evidence-based, potential treatments that include psychotherapy, yoga, and avoidance of caffeine. These alternative therapies may assist in treating OCD symptoms by helping a person feel calmer, but they are not typically helpful in addressing the underlying causes of the disorder. Penzel said, "Medication and behavior therapy are still the gold standard, and they still get the most people better."[49]

Penzel recommended not giving up on medication and behavior therapy, even if at first it appears that these are not producing the desired results. "Often when people say a treatment doesn't work for them, you dig a little further, and you find out that it just wasn't administered the best way possible," he said. "Just because they haven't had a good treatment experience doesn't mean that nothing can help them, or that treatment doesn't work."[50]

INPATIENT THERAPY

When someone has not found relief through medications and outpatient therapy, and their OCD is severely impacting their life, an option for further help is a residential treatment facility that specializes in OCD. This is also an option for people who live far from experienced treatment providers. Residential treatment facilities offer intensive inpatient treatment for a period that generally lasts one to three months.

Psychiatrist Michael A. Jenike helped start the Obsessive Compulsive Disorder Institute (OCDI) at McLean Hospital in Belmont, Massachusetts, in 1997. This was the first residential treatment center that focused solely on OCD. He explained why such facilities are necessary:

> *In my opinion, the treatment of OCD is quite unique. Many severely ill OCD patients had been hospitalized in general psychiatric units; and most were not helped or even got worse. Psychiatric hospitalization is a huge blow to one's self-esteem and should only be considered when other treatments have failed. If an OCD patient is put into a general psychiatric unit that does not know how to treat OCD or is not behaviorally oriented, patients feel worse and even more like a failure.*[51]

A typical inpatient program includes medication, ERP, and individual and group therapy. Since OCD involves a wide range of symptom types, some programs divide patients into support groups consisting of people who are experiencing similar symptoms. Psychologist Deborah Osgood Hynes of the OCDI reported:

> *Symptom-specific groups allow people to discuss issues that they may not feel comfortable discussing in a larger group context with others that are not experiencing those symptoms. In these groups it is not uncommon to hear people say that for the first time they have met someone struggling with issues just like them and were able to face issues of shame or embarrassment.*[52]

A RARE THERAPY

One form of therapy that is sometimes used for the most severe, treatment-resistant OCD is called deep brain stimulation (DBS). In this type of medical therapy, two electrodes are surgically implanted in brain areas that have been identified as having a role in OCD. The electrodes are connected by wires under the skin to tiny devices that generate electrical pulses, which stimulate the brain. Doctors control the pulse generators with a hand-held device or computer. One worldwide study showed that out of 26 patients who were diagnosed with treatment-resistant OCD, 61.5 percent had a positive response to DBS. While this response rate is similar to other neurosurgeries, it is difficult to draw a real comparison with such a small sample size.

The FDA has approved the use of DBS for treatment-resistant OCD under a Humanitarian Device Exemption (HDE). This approval requires careful monitoring in the number of patients that can be tested. In addition, the procedure must be done at an institution with previous DBS experience because the placement of electrodes and the amount of stimulation given is crucial. Most people with OCD will never be recommended for this type of therapy, as medication and ERP control the vast majority of cases.

ADVANCING KNOWLEDGE

As more medical research is done, more answers about the causes and effective treatments for OCD are emerging. Dr. David Rosenberg, chair of psychiatry and behavioral neurosciences for the Wayne State University School of Medicine, and his colleagues at Wayne State University and the Detroit Medical Center's Children's Hospital of Michigan say that children with different OCD symptoms also have

OCD can appear at any age, but it typically develops either before age 12 or after age 17.

distinctly different brain patterns, indicating that there may be several subtypes of OCD. "For example, Rosenberg and colleagues have found significantly different brain patterns in children with OCD who repetitively wash their hands than in children with OCD who repetitively check to make sure the door is locked. 'We see different things in the brain, and they respond differently to treatment,'"[53] according to Rosenberg.

The team's study of MRIs in children with OCD showed evidence of an imbalance of glutamate, which, according to Rosenberg, acts as a light switch for the brain. He said, "The key is that the light switch of the brain isn't working properly and that just causes the whole system to go haywire, misfire … Instead of getting the signal that 'Okay, I'm safe now,' children with OCD get the signal that things are getting much more dangerous and unsafe."[54]

Further research and clinical trials in the use of glutamate-targeted medications for treatment-resistant OCD have begun across the United States based on the research of Rosenberg and his team. Although it takes time for new research to result in new methods, some new treatments are now available.

COMBATING MISINFORMATION

Some people believe mental illness helps people create art, which may cause some people to feel they need to be without medication or therapy in order to create. John Green, author of *Turtles All the Way Down*, a book in which the main character has OCD, has been open about his own struggle with anxiety and OCD and wrote about this belief in an article for the website *Medium*:

> *Mental illness is stigmatized, but it is also romanticized. If you google the phrase "all artists are," the first suggestion is "mad." We hear that genius is next to insanity; we see Carrie Mathison on [the television show]* Homeland *going off her meds so that she can discover the identity of the terrorists and save America.*
>
> *Of course, there are kernels of truth here: Many artists and storytellers do live with mental illness. But many don't. And what I want to say today I guess is that you can be sane and be an artist, and also that if you are sick, getting help—although it is hard and exhausting and inexcusably difficult to access—will not make you less of an artist.*[1]

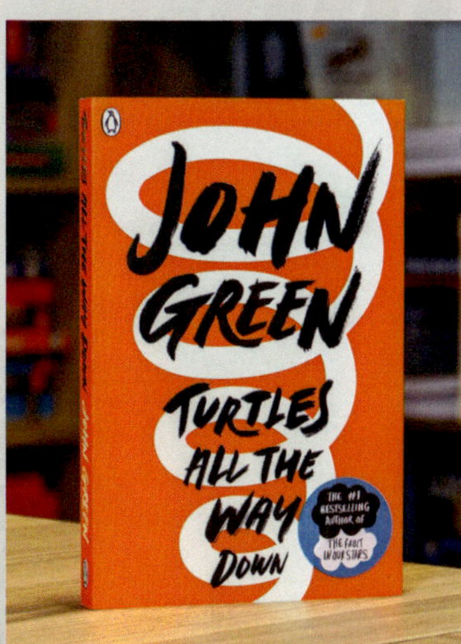

John Green drew on his personal experiences with OCD to write *Turtles All the Way Down*.

1. John Green, "My NerdCon Stories Talk about Mental Illness and Creativity," *Medium*, October 15, 2016. medium.com/@johngreen/my-nerdcon-stories-talk-about-mental-illness-and-creativity-bfac9c29387e.

Some therapists have started using drugs that target glutamate, such as ketamine, to treat OCD. Ketamine has a history of use as an illegal party drug, but recent research has found that small doses in controlled settings provide nearly instant relief for many people with depression and OCD. As medical research continues, more and better treatments will likely become available in the future.

LIVING WELL WITH OCD

According to some estimates, it can take an average of 14 years before someone's OCD is correctly diagnosed and treated. Once someone finds the right treatment for them, their life can completely change. Their symptoms will likely flare up from time to time, especially when external stressors are present. Times of widespread uncertainty, such as the COVID-19 pandemic, can cause OCD symptoms to return even when someone has had them under control for a long time. Understanding that both internal and external factors can contribute to OCD is a crucial part of managing the disorder well.

Despite the risk of flare-ups, people with OCD often live happy, healthy, and productive lives when their symptoms are managed. Therapy, medication, and a strong support network can make flare-ups easier to deal with. Treatment helps people with OCD learn healthy ways to cope with their disorder. For example, instead of ruminating about whether a friend is mad at them, a person with OCD might make a conscious effort to think, 'Maybe she is and maybe she isn't. If she tells me she's mad, I'll deal with it then,' and turn their focus to an activity that brings them joy, such as exercising or painting. The distress of dealing with the uncertainty without turning to compulsions will linger for a little while, but it will be overcome faster and more effectively than it would by performing compulsions. Having OCD does not have to stop someone from going to new places, meeting new people, or having exciting life experiences.

Once considered a rare diagnosis, today if someone were to search "obsessive-compulsive disorder" on the internet, the results would be hundreds of articles about new discoveries in OCD research and treatment, personal stories, and places to find support. The IOCDF continues to spread awareness by establishing an International OCD Awareness Week. Recognized annually around the world every second week in October, events during International OCD Awareness Week include OCD screening exams, conferences, lectures, and fundraisers. Contests have been held since 2014 to encourage people to keep the public conversation going about OCD through creative expression. In 2017, the organization held an inaugural OCD Capital Walk to increase awareness about OCD as well as provide information on resources for OCD. Each year, it also holds a YouTube Challenge to spread awareness of the disorder through storytelling or art.

For many years, people with OCD were misunderstood by the public. To admit to the unexplainable, irrational urges and the embarrassing, unending cycle of compulsions was to carry the burden of a social stigma. Through continued awareness, research, and development into OCD treatment, some of this stigma has lessened in recent years. Society and loved ones can further help support those with OCD and end the stigma around OCD and mental illnesses in general with their support and understanding.

NOTES

INTRODUCTION: INTRUSIVE THOUGHTS

1. Quoted in Kristen Fuller, "A True Story of Living with Obsessive-Compulsive Disorder," *Psychology Today*, April 3, 2017. www.psychologytoday.com/blog/happiness-is-state-mind/201704/true-story-living-obsessive-compulsive-disorder.
2. Quoted in Fuller, "A True Story of Living with Obsessive-Compulsive Disorder."
3. Tiffany Dawn Hasse, "Transmuting Pain into Art," The OCD Stories, March 20, 2017. theocdstories.com/ocd/transmuting-pain-into-art/.

CHAPTER ONE: OBSESSIONS AND COMPULSIONS

4. "About OCD," International OCD Foundation, accessed September 9, 2017. iocdf.org/about-OCD/#obsessions.
5. Fred Penzel, *Obsessive-Compulsive Disorder: A Complete Guide to Getting Well and Staying Well.* New York, NY: Oxford University Press, 2000, p. 212.
6. Quoted in Michael Knisley, "The Biggest Save," *The Sporting News*, March 6, 1995.
7. Penzel, *Obsessive-Compulsive Disorder*, p. 266.
8. Liz, interview by Jacqueline Adams, March 15, 2007.

9. Quoted in "Psychiatry: Obsessive-Compulsive and Related Disorders Research Program," Stanford School of Medicine, 2007. ocd.stanford.edu/treatment/history.html.

10. Quoted in "Psychiatry: Obsessive-Compulsive and Related Disorders Research Program."

11. John Bunyan, *Grace Abounding to the Chief of Sinners: A Brief Relation of the Exceeding Mercy of God in Christ to His Poor Servant*. Third Millennium Press, 2017.

12. Quoted in Judith L. Rapaport, *The Boy Who Couldn't Stop Washing: The Experience and Treatment of Obsessive-Compulsive Disorder*. New York, NY: Signet, 1989, pp. 4–5.

13. Raymond D. Fowler, "Howard Hughes: A Psychological Autopsy," *Psychology Today*, May 1986.

14. Quoted in Rapoport, *The Boy Who Couldn't Stop Washing*, p. 15.

15. Rapoport, *The Boy Who Couldn't Stop Washing*, p. 8.

16. Quoted in Rapoport, *The Boy Who Couldn't Stop Washing*, p. 14.

17. Quoted in Richard Swinson, ed., et al, *Obsessive-Compulsive Disorder: Theory, Research, and Treatment*. New York, NY: The Guilford Press, 1998, p. 368.

18. Corey Hirsch, "Dark, Dark, Dark, Dark, Dark, Dark, Dark, Dark," *The Players' Tribune*, February 15, 2017. www.theplayerstribune.com/corey-hirsch-dark-dark-dark/.

19. Hirsch, "Dark, Dark, Dark, Dark, Dark, Dark, Dark, Dark."

CHAPTER TWO: DIAGNOSING OCD

20. "Comedian Maria Bamford Finds Humor in Uncomfortable Topics," NPR, May 27, 2016. www.npr.org/2016/05/27/479593625/comedian-maria-bamford-finds-humor-in-uncomfortable-topics.
21. Penzel, *Obsessive-Compulsive Disorder*, p. 54.
22. Chrissie Hodges, "4 Unique Challenges when Your Compulsions Are All in Your Mind," The Mighty, January 29, 2016. themighty.com/2016/01/4-unique-challenges-when-your-compulsions-are-all-in-your-mind/.
23. Steven Taylor, "Assessment of OCD," in *Obsessive-Compulsive Disorder: Theory, Research, and Treatment*. New York, NY: Guilford Press, 1998, p. 250.
24. Jim Hatton, interview by Jacqueline Adams, April 4, 2007.
25. Hatton, interview.

CHAPTER THREE: OCD'S EFFECTS

26. Diance, "Living with OCD: One Woman's Story," Anxiety and Depression Association of America, accessed September 11, 2017. www.adaa.org/living-with-anxiety/personal-stories/living-with-ocd-one-womans-story.
27. Diance, "Living with OCD."
28. Hatton, interview.
29. Quoted in Penzel, *Obsessive-Compulsive Disorder*, p. 268.

30. Samantha Gluck, "OCD and Depression, OCD and Anxiety, OCD and ADHD," HealthyPlace, February 3, 2017. www.healthyplace.com/ocd-related-disorders/ocd/ocd-and-depression-ocd-and-anxiety-ocd-and-adhd/.
31. Penzel, *Obsessive-Compulsive Disorder*, p. 303.
32. Quoted in Herbert L. Gravitz, *Obsessive-Compulsive Disorder: New Help for the Family*. Santa Barbara, CA: Healing Visions Press, p. 15.
33. Gail Steketee and Nina A. Pruyn, "Families of Individuals with Obsessive-Compulsive Disorder," in *Obsessive-Compulsive Disorder: Theory, Research, and Treatment*, Richard P. Swinson, et al., ed., p. 124.
34. Rapoport, *The Boy Who Couldn't Stop Washing*, p. 91.
35. Rapoport, *The Boy Who Couldn't Stop Washing*, p. 91.
36. Steketee and Pruyn, "Families of Individuals with Obsessive-Compulsive Disorder," p. 121.
37. Steketee and Pruyn, "Families of Individuals with Obsessive-Compulsive Disorder," p. 130.

CHAPTER FOUR: TREATMENT OPTIONS

38. Jim Hatton, email interview by Jacqueline Adams, June 1, 2007.
39. Gail Steketee and Teresa Pigott, *Obsessive Compulsive Disorder: The Latest Assessment and Treatment Strategies*. Kansas City, MO: Compact Clinicals, 2006, p. 56.
40. Hatton, email interview.

41. Steketee and Pigott, *Obsessive Compulsive Disorder*, p. 67.
42. Teresa A. Pigott and Sheila Seay, "Biological Treatments for Obsessive-Compulsive Disorder," in *Obsessive-Compulsive Disorder: Theory, Research, and Treatment*, Richard P. Swinson, et al., ed., p. 315.
43. Ben Martin, "In-Depth: Cognitive Behavioral Therapy," PsychCentral, May 17, 2016. psychcentral.com/lib/in-depth-cognitive-behavioral-therapy/.
44. Hatton, interview.
45. Hatton, email interview.
46. Fred Penzel, interview by Jacqueline Adams, May 16, 2007.
47. Hatton, interview.

CHAPTER FIVE: LIVING WITH OCD

48. Hatton, email interview.
49. Penzel, interview.
50. Penzel, interview.
51. Quoted in "OCF Intensive Treatment Program Interviews," International OCD Foundation. www.ocfoundation.org/ocd-intensivetreatment-programs.html.
52. Deborah Osgood-Hynes, "Facing Fears," *OCD Newsletter*, Late Fall 2005, p. 11.
53. Eric M. Strauss and Alexia Valiente, "New Distinction of OCD Subtypes May Benefit Future Diagnosis, Treatment," ABC News, May 23, 2014. abcnews.go.com/Health/distinction-ocd-subtypes-benefit-future-diagnosis-treatment/story?id=23842030.

54. Strauss and Valiente, "New Distinction of OCD Subtypes."

GLOSSARY

amygdala: One of the structures that make up the basal ganglia; responsible for signaling fear.

autoimmune response: A reaction in which the immune system mistakes body cells for invaders and attacks them.

basal ganglia: Brain area that triggers and controls voluntary movement.

behavioral avoidance tests (BATs): Tests that measure a patient's levels of fear and avoidance.

body dysmorphic disorder (BDD): Strong, persistent preoccupation with an imagined or slight physical defect.

cognitive behavioral therapy (CBT): A way of treating psychological problems by identifying negative thoughts and replacing them with positive ones.

deep brain stimulation (DBS): A type of neurosurgery in which electrodes are implanted in the brain.

magnetic resonance imaging (MRI): A type of imaging study that uses a magnetic field and sound waves to create a computerized image.

neuron: A nerve cell.

neurosurgery: Surgery involving the brain or nervous system.

neurotransmitter: A chemical messenger that delivers signals from one neuron to the next.

orbitofrontal cortex: Part of the brain's frontal lobes; organizes and interprets information.

serotonin: A type of neurotransmitter believed to be involved with OCD and other mental illnesses, such as depression.

Subjective Units of Distress Scale (SUDS): A scale ranging from 0 to 100 that patients use to rate how much anxiety a situation would provoke.

thalamus: A brain area that receives and transmits messages from one brain area to another.

therapist: A person who is trained and licensed in a particular type of treatment.

ORGANIZATIONS TO CONTACT

Anxiety Disorders Association of America (ADAA)
8701 Georgia Avenue
Suite 412
Silver Spring, MD 20910
www.adaa.org
Instagram: anxietyanddepression_adaa
YouTube: ADAA_Anxiety
This organization educates professionals and the public about OCD and other anxiety disorders, helps people find treatment providers and support groups, and encourages research into causes and treatment.

International OCD Foundation (IOCDF)
P.O. Box 961029
Boston, MA 02196
iocdf.org
Instagram: iocdf
YouTube: IOCDF
The many activities of this organization include educating the public and treatment providers about OCD and related disorders, organizing support groups, supporting research into causes and treatments, and maintaining a list of providers across the United States who treat OCD.

Mental Health America
500 Montgomery Street
Suite 820
Alexandria, VA 22314
mhanational.org
Instagram: mentalhealthamerica
YouTube: mentalhealthamerica
This organization's mission is to educate the public about mental health, fight for equal and appropriate mental health care for all people, and provide support to people living with mental health issues or substance abuse problems.

National Alliance on Mental Illness (NAMI)
3803 N. Fairfax Dr., Suite 100
Arlington, VA 22203
helpline: 1-800-950-6264
www.nami.org
Instagram: namicommunicate
TikTok: nami
YouTube: NAMICommunicate
NAMI is a national nonprofit outreach, educational, and advocacy organization dedicated to improving the lives of people with mental illnesses and their families. People who need mental health support can call NAMI's helpline or visit their website to chat or text a professional.

FOR MORE INFORMATION

BOOKS

Blohm, Craig E. *Managing OCD.* San Diego, CA: ReferencePoint Press, 2022.

Cooke, Pan. *Puzzled: A Memoir of Growing Up with OCD.* New York, NY: Rocky Pond Books, 2024.

Ellis, Mary Beth, and Anne S. Walters. *Obsessive-Compulsive and Related Disorders.* Hollywood, FL: Mason Crest, 2023.

Hall, Hazel. *A Kids Book about OCD.* New York, NY: DK Publishing, 2024.

Hershfield, Jon. *The OCD Workbook for Teens: Mindfulness & CBT Skills to Help You Overcome Unwanted Thoughts and Compulsions.* Oakland, CA: Instant Help Books, 2021.

Huston, Jimmy. *The OCD Funbook: Really?* Los Angeles, CA: Cosworth Publishing, 2023.

Kant, Jared Douglas, Martin Franklin, and Linda Wasmer Andrews. *The Thought that Counts: A Firsthand Account of One Teenager's Experience with Obsessive-Compulsive Disorder.* New York, NY: Oxford University Press, 2023.

WEBSITES

Intrusive Thoughts
www.intrusivethoughts.org
Founded by someone with OCD, this website explains the different types of intrusive thoughts someone with OCD might have as well as personal accounts of how people have dealt with their OCD. This resource helps people without OCD learn what the illness is like and helps people with OCD see that they are not alone.

NOCD
www.treatmyocd.com/learn/blog
This website provides a wealth of information about what OCD is, what obsessions and compulsions can look like in different people, and tips for overcoming obsessive thoughts without performing compulsions.

The OCD Stories
theocdstories.com
This website hosts a podcast that discusses symptoms and treatment of OCD to provide support and a community for those with the disorder.

INDEX

E

F

G

H

N

O

P

PHOTO CREDITS

Cover, Srdjan Randjelovic/Shutterstock.com; cover, pp. 1-104 Trisno Wardana/Shutterstock.com; cover, pp. 1,3 ,4, 6, 10, 25, 37, 43, 73, 84, 90, 92, 94, 96, 103, 104 Sentavio/Shutterstock.com; p. 7 pixelheadphoto digitalskillet/Shutterstock.com; p. 9 New Africa/ Shutterstock.com; p. 14 Alexey Rotanov/Shutterstock.com; p. 20 Tanyastock/Shutterstock.com; p. 23 Perfect Wave/ Shutterstock.com; p. 31 Pheelings media/Shutterstock.com; p. 33 Doucefleur/Shutteratock.com; p. 34 Pixel-Shot/Shutterstock.com; p. 36 AstroStar/Shutterstock.com; p. 38 Rawpixel.com/Shutterstock.com; p. 39 tetxu/ Shutterstock.com; p. 40 Prostock-studio/Shutterstock.com; p. 41 Srdjan Randjelovic/Shutterstock.com; p. 45 Monkey Business Images/Shutterstock.com; p. 49 fizkes/ Shutterstock.com; p. 51 Macrovector/Shutterstock.com; p. 55 Corona Borealis Studio/Shutterstock.com; p. 57 Sonis Photography/Shutterstock.com; p. 60 PeopleImages.com - Yuri A/Shutterstock.com; p. 61 Yiistocking/Shutterstock.com; p. 63 My July/Shutterstock.com; p. 67 verbaska/ Shutterstock.com; p.68 STEKLO/Shutterstock.com; p. 71 Andrey_Popov/Shutterstock.com; p. 74 wavebreakmedia/ Shutterstock.com; p. 75 Media_Photos/Shutterstock.com; p. 80 triocean/Shutterstock.com; p. 81 hamdi bendali/ Shutterstock.com.

ABOUT THE AUTHOR

JENNIFER LOMBARDO earned her BA in English from the University at Buffalo and still resides in Buffalo, New York, with her cat, Chip. She has helped write a number of books for young adults, on topics ranging from world history to body image. In her spare time, she enjoys cross-stitching, hiking, and volunteering with Habitat for Humanity.